DIPLOMAS IN MUSIC

DIPLOMAS
IN MUSIC

T. C. L. PRITCHARD

M.A., MUS.D., F.R.C.O.,
L.R.A.M., A.R.C.M.

CRESCENDO PUBLISHING COMPANY
Boston

Standard Book Number 87597-003-6
Library of Congress Card Number 68-59103
Printed in the United States of America
Copyright © T. C. L. Pritchard 1960

Preface

AT the examinations for L.R.A.M., A.R.C.M., the Royal College of Organists, Trinity College, and other diplomas in music, hundreds of candidates fail each year to satisfy the requirements. This accumulating toll of frustrated hopes shows that for the great majority of entrants the lessons it instils continue to remain unlearned.

The following pages are the results of many years of experience in dealing with these examinations, and are intended to help students to avoid the unnecessary difficulties and disappointments arising from mistaken views and inadequate preparation.

The essential qualities combined with methods of work which can lead to success are proclaimed through the treatment of each diploma. They cannot be repeated often enough, and if they do not appear on every page they are certainly implied. On them alone must be based the effort for what is worth striving for, and to them is due its value when it has been attained.

T. C. L. PRITCHARD.

Contents

Introduction

THE value to the student of preparing for a musical diploma lies in its being an impetus to work along established lines, and in its making him undertake certain necessary aspects of his subject which otherwise he might tend to neglect. It affords him the advantage of a discipline over himself by which he goes beyond what is actually required. When it has been achieved the diploma is a guarantee of work well done on a sure foundation, certifying the holder to be not only a solid but a practical musician. Further than that it does not go—such as to suggest that as a pianist he is inevitably an organist, or as a violinist a choir conductor. It applies only to his particular subject and invests him with an authority to pursue it before the public. But whatever benefit it may bring him in the competition of his profession, it has opened before him an expanding world of musical interest and furnished him with the means to explore it for himself.

Most candidates are presumably convinced that they are ready for the examination, otherwise they would not be candidates. Yet as a general rule a large proportion of them are unsuccessful. Among them are even those who having conscientiously prepared themselves ought to have passed, if only they had exercised more care : sad it is that what has been done at home should be undone in the examination room. For the rest, some enter with only a slight idea of what is expected of them. Others are projected by complacency : someone they know has achieved the diploma, and they should be able to do likewise. Many more have not learned to work ; they are under a curious delusion that the examination is easier than it is, and they rely on their teachers to help them to scrape a way through. And there are others who go in hoping for the best, which may be no more than passing in a section of it and the remainder they will complete at some future date. Or it may even be to gain experience for trying the whole thing all over again.

Most of these people are in the position of having little or no musical background in their home lives. They have been imbued with no tradition that it was a subject of consideration: they were born with no respect for it. They were allowed to drift into a taste for what is poor. Then suddenly they allowed themselves the luxury of envying the pleasure and fortune music seemed to bring to certain people, and having by some obscure reasoning decided it is a sort of soft option, they must adopt it and go the whole way to the sanction of a diploma— or degree, as they call it: they must take 'their letters.' It will give them a standing, though they have nothing to stand on. Yet how are they to be convinced of their great advantage and of the difficulty of their rising above it? They have far more to do than they can imagine. They should have to go back to the very beginning and form a tradition for themselves. But never could they believe that to be necessary. They can tinkle their slipshod numbers well enough, and it is only a matter of changing them for others.

Yet a few there continue to be who have sentimental ideas that the difficulties under which they labour may be appreciated by the kind hearts of the examiners and lead them to make sympathetic allowances. Perhaps the examiners may have a pass to spare and bestow it on a deserving student. But whatever troubles he may have to discourage him—be they lack of time or money, domestic or bread-winning complications, perhaps poor health, and sometimes he may seem to have more than his share—the examiners cannot and ought not to know of them, and if they did they would not be influenced by them. They are there to judge by results, however dearly bought, and on them alone must they make a decision.

Most of the entrants for these examinations have little conception of system in their preparation, and they have no standard of attainment beyond their own insular ones. Certain of the tests they dislike and so they neglect them. There are too many scales: the aural tests are meaningless. The pieces they are satisfied to play as correctly as they can in the same slow, dull way and nothing more. They have developed neither intelligence nor imagination. The spirit of music they have missed and they have no thrill to declare. In the paper-work, they may not take the precaution to understand a question in their own language: they read it casually, conceive it to be a different question, and so spend valuable time in giving the wrong answer. Or they may show the same irresponsibility in transposition, in ornaments, and in harmony, all simple enough if scrupulously treated. To these people the examination and the result that follows are a salutary reminder of realities.

Every good diploma examination is framed as a warfare against carelessness. This has been forced upon it by the candidates themselves, and as their carelessness continues the examination tends year by year to become more difficult. The most profitable preparation for it is to be found in undergoing local examinations of a reputable kind. These rise by successive grades through the various subjects of paper-work, playing at sight, aural tests, scales, studies, and pieces, so as to lead with the final one to what is required of them for the diploma. The student may start with whatever grade suits his capabilities. An important point is that the grading is carefully and effectively arranged to pass from one step to another; but of still more importance is the experience he will gain of undergoing examination before different examiners and the increasing confidence he will acquire in doing for them work which is clearly outlined and he knows to be within his powers. He will learn that however well he has prepared himself he must prove it by attention and resource. At the same time he must not conclude that after passing with honours the so-called final grade the diploma is only a corresponding grade higher. The diploma is a much greater step forward: the final grade is on an amateur, the diploma on a professional, standard of efficiency.

The examination for every diploma consists of two parts, the paper-work and a series of practical tests. These vary with different institutions, but, taking the paper-work first, it generally comprises rudiments of music, aural tests, harmony, form, analysis, and fingering of set passages.

The Paper Work

THE RUDIMENTS OF MUSIC

THE rudiments of music have innumerable subtleties and anomalies which call for imagination as well as knowledge, and they must be mastered by the student by going through a reliable book and, after reading each over several times, answering all its questions and doing all its exercises. Frequent revision of essential points is of the first importance. Then the corresponding questions in previous papers of the examination should be worked with the same care, noting the times they require and practising the urgent matter of speed until they are well within the proportionate time out of the customary allowance of three hours. In this as in everything else he must be thorough in preparation and leave nothing to chance.

The writing must be clear and tidy—in ink and not ball-point pen, the details of notation exact, every black note a spot and not a stroke, every minim head round and with its accidental honestly on line or in space, its dot only in a space, and if a note through alteration should become illegible its alphabetical letter should be inserted above; a slur or tie should rise from and fall to the head or tail of a particular note; the horizontal line of a group of quavers or semiquavers should be drawn across the lines of the stave rather than along them—all as much in the interest of the candidate as for the comfort of the examiners.

The general tests in intervals would not give trouble if it were recalled that a major or perfect interval is one in which the upper note is in the major scale of the lower note, and the numerical value of an interval is reckoned by the number of lines and spaces it occupies, counting those on which its two notes stand. The quality of an interval away from its context is not to be judged by its sound; an augmented fifth, for instance, sounds the same as a minor sixth. Another point is that such an interval as C sharp to F double sharp remains numerically the same if we take a sharp from each note, making it C to F sharp, and so an augmented fourth. The adding of an interval below a note requires more thought than one above it. It has to be remembered that, as with one above, the given note must not be altered. For instance: write a minor seventh below G. A seventh below G is bound to be A something; the major key that has G for its seventh note is A flat; A flat to G is a major seventh, and so the note wanted is A natural. Or it might be done indirectly: as a major seventh above A is G sharp, a minor seventh is therefore G natural. Again, write a diminished fourth below G. A fourth below is bound to be D something; D to G is a perfect fourth and a diminished one will be a semitone less and therefore D sharp.

A simple method of handling the chromatic scale is to remember that in the harmonic form, both ascending and descending, the first and fifth notes of the major scale appear only once, the others twice: the plain notes in that order should be written out first and then the necessary accidentals inserted. In the ascending melodic form the third and seventh notes appear only once, the others twice; the descending form is the same as the harmonic. Another useful fact to know about the harmonic chromatic scale is that if to the notes of the major scale are added the other ones in the two tonic minor scales, two notes remain to be filled in to complete the chromatic scale, a second and a fourth, of which the second has to be flattened and the fourth sharpened. And so to such a question as 'In what scale does the interval A flat to C sharp appear?' the answer is the harmonic chromatic of G. This formation of the scale provides ready answers to all questions dealing with chromatic intervals.

In such a matter as transferring from close score to separate parts, it must be remembered that the C clefs are used in the inner parts, or if for open vocal score that the treble clef is employed for the three upper parts while the tenor notes are written an octave higher than they sound. If the arrangement is for string quartet, the alto C clef is reserved for the viola and the bowing, which differs from phrasing, must be inserted; a perusal of a miniature quartet score by Haydn or Mozart will show how this is done. Each note, its stem up or down as it is below or above the middle line, should be vertical with its corresponding ones in the other parts above and below; so that if ornaments are to be written out, they should be done first to find where the chordings are due. Special care is necessary as to accidentals not repeated in short score but now requiring to be so in the separate parts. For instance, if this fragment is to be put into open score:

the first alto note will be a seventh above middle C, the tenor a fourth above, and so the passage will be written as:

The soprano B and the tenor B of the second chord in the two-stave original are flat notes because of the flats in the first chord. But in open score these flats have no influence outside their own staves, and consequently they must be repeated in the second chord.

Transposition into another key is one of the most fruitful opportunities for carelessness and carries with it heavier penalties. First of all the key of the given passage must be found by recalling that the chromatic notes are usually auxiliary ones a semitone above or below the actual notes of the key; this semitone characteristic prevails even when the chromatic notes are approached by leap. Eliminating these and considering the other notes as diatonic, the key may be found. A false step here may make the whole thing wrong. If the transposition is to be in open score with C clefs, it should be done at once, not outlined in the treble and bass and then rewritten in the C clefs, which is a great waste of time. It is essential to see at the very beginning that the intervals above or below are correctly placed relatively to middle C: otherwise again not a mark of credit will it bring. It will be found that if the tenor part has a treble substituted for the C clef, it will have its part transposed, as it happens, a ninth higher, with two sharps more or two flats less. If we take this in the key of F:

a ninth higher is G and so the tenor part as a treble will be in that key. (The only divergence is when an accidental appears, but it can be mentally verified. Here the two tenor crotchets are a tone apart, and so in G the natural will be understood as a sharp.) This is less complicated than it sounds and it can be reassuring, for if it is correct in G it will be so with the C clef. But in the act of transposing the chief trouble lies in the chromatic notes, and these are best handled by observing the separate numerical intervals in each original part and adding the particular accidentals they require. The whole procedure calls for much vigilance, and sometimes the marks allotted to it are not commensurate with the time it entails.

Few aspects of the rudiments paper contain more danger than the writing out of ornaments, generally again because of lack of care. The performance of these embellishments is easier than their indication in notation, though there can be different opinions on their interpretation according to their period or context. But for examination purposes the use of the general rules is what is expected, and for that certain considerations can very desirably save time. An acciaccatura to a crochet, for instance, 𝅘, is written down at once as two half-notes, 𝅗, and for every short stroke to the stem of the first note is added a dot to the head of the second; and so it will be 𝅗 or 𝅗, according to the speed of the piece. It is a simple arithmetical fact that in every case the two notes amount, as they must do, to the exact value of the note which has the ornament. If this note is a quaver, we begin with two semiquavers; if it is a dotted crotchet or a minim, we regard it at first as a crotchet and tie the second note to what remains of its value; e.g. 𝅘. will be 𝅗. If an acciaccatura, or equally for that matter an appoggiatura, be attached to one note of a chord, it is important to remember, not only that the other notes remain unaffected by the ornament, but in addition that they come in with it and not with the second note. Thus: 𝅘 will be written as 𝅘. Special care is necessary in the two different cases of an acciaccatura and an appoggiatura when the chord is an arpeggio.

An upper or lower mordent is treated on the same principles as the acciaccatura, but consists of three notes instead of two. That is, if the principal note is a crotchet we begin with ♫♪ and for every stroke added to the stems of the first two notes we add a dot to the third: thus ♫♪⋯. In considering a trill it should be scarcely necessary to say that the notes forming it must when reckoned up amount to the value of the note which bears it. And yet often this is unfulfilled: it is irksome work counting them and so is frivolously done. It can be simplified for the candidate and made clearer for the examiner to read if long series of notes are shown in groups, such as ♬♬ ♬♬. The beginning and the end of a trill require more consideration than they generally get. If it begins with the upper note the number of notes in the trill will be even, if with the lower note it will be odd. When at the end the trill has a triplet, the triplet will not be at the very end but on the penultimate half or quarter beat, according to the speed. The turn, like many other ornaments, represents pictorially what it stands for, as when we make a graph through the heads of its notes we get the sign, thus: ♫. The distinction between the usual form ∾ and its inversion ∿ is sometimes overlooked, and one way to impress it on the mind is to associate the usual form with some natural action, such as a flourish at the end of a letter ((⌒)). An important matter connected with this ornament, as with the others, lies in an accidental it may entail, and especially the fact that its influence continues and may have to be cancelled before the bar is finished. For instance, in writing out ♫ a natural must be placed before the F. This unhappily is also often overlooked.

AURAL TESTS

Next in rising importance in the examination requirements are the tests in ear training, for they are founded on the rudiments and they are the foundation of the harmony work. Many candidates underestimate them and fail: a number pass in everything but them and have the additional expense of time and of money preparing to undergo them again, sometimes more than once; some in the end lose heart and give up all further thought of the diploma. What a futile climax to the rest of their good work! For anyone who has successfully taken the practical part and the paper work is bound to have done a lot of ear testing and criticizing of himself. And so it is the melancholy fact that the little that remains to be done may cost what is out of all proportion to its elementary nature or the few minutes it occupies in the examination.

To the really musical student this should be inconceivable. Instinctively does he give himself tests beyond any that are necessary: he makes them part of his daily life. And so must everyone. Even when one who has not the natural initiative to do so seeks assistance in acquiring it, an hour's lesson each week is not affording him anything like enough for his purpose. He has to go far beyond it by doing the greater part to help himself. He must make a habit of listening. Whether at church, a concert, or by radio, everything he hears he must make an ear test. A simple knowledge of sol-fa is a great aid in mentally seeing sounds as they should be written down and in mentally hearing what is actually written down. His necessary familiarity with the scales gives him a start in developing his sense of pitch, and practice on the piano, which will be the instrument used at the examination, will improve every aspect of it. It will show him the unquestionable difference in character between a major interval and a minor one, between a consonant and a dissonant one. It will make him aware that *mfs* is not the same as *ltd'*, that neither of them is the same as *drm.* It will help him in discriminating the various times and their signatures, which he knows from the rudiments; his counting will reveal the variations of rhythm, and with it he should know how to beat time in the usual conducting style. His own pieces and everything else within reach will add to this experience. But more than anything will a hymn-book provide profitable practice in playing its familiar melodies, then repeating and writing them out away from the book, trying to hear unfamiliar ones, proving their correctness by playing them over and memorizing them. Similarly with reading over alto, tenor, and bass parts separately. From that he can begin to discriminate between two notes sounded together, leading to two moving parts and ultimately on to two melodic phrases of distinctive character together, simple and short at first. At odd moments, at leisure or while travelling, he can mentally go over intervals and rhythms, familiar phrases he has memorized, unfamiliar ones that come to him, and picture them as written out— doing as much as he can to ear test himself.

Then will come the particular features of major and minor triads and their inversions, from the sound of which on the piano it should be impossible to confuse one with another. It will be noted that an augmented triad with its totally different personality consists of two major thirds, a diminished one of two minor thirds, that if the top note of a major triad be raised a semitone the result is an augmented triad, while if the root is so raised the result is a diminished triad; on the other hand, if the top note of the minor triad be lowered a semitone the result is a diminished triad, while if the root is so lowered it is an augmented triad. Specially to be recognized are the very appreciable differences between these triads in close positions and in open ones. From that progress is made to four-part chords and their change of character with distribution of the parts. Here the hymn-book supplies all that is required. A habit of noticing the movement of the bass—a greater difficulty for women than for men because it is outside their singing experience—will show the nature of the chords and distinguish cadences. This leads to modulations, which should have a physical effect on the sensitive ear as it traces what new chromatic note is introduced, in what part it appears, and to what key it leads; when the chromatic influence is withdrawn and a return is made to the original key. It can be a very pleasant recreation.

At the examination the candidate must be fully alert in attentively listening and acting at once in the limited time. He should at one hearing memorize the test so as to be able to repeat it independently and he must mentally see it. In dealing with triads, the only difficulty possible should be in open as compared with close positions. Some candidates are known to guess the position correctly as open, but when asked what is the middle note they name it according to the close position; which is of course carelessness and rightly costs a few marks. When a melodic phrase is to be written down, it is most important that the degree of the scale on which it begins should be carefully decided, for from it rightly or wrongly progress the intervals between the other notes. The candidate should have pencil in hand ready to outline on the stave with plain dots the positions of the notes while the other hand is marking the rhythm. On no account should time be wasted by rubbing out: simply strike out.

Suppose the phrase is the opening one of Haydn's Austrian hymn and that it is unfamiliar to him. He is told the key is F: down goes the flat on B—no clef; anything to save time. He must immediately put down what he thinks—write something. Evidently begins on *d*: the next two above, back one, up to C—no, only one between—B, next two down, leap one and *d*. C and straight down the scale, five notes—but it should not get to *d—dmsl*, D is the note, strike out: D to G, one up, leap down one and up to B—B right? *dms*—no, it is *s*—C.

It is being played again: verify. Left hand says 1 2 *and* 3, so add in own shorthand dotted F, quaver G, and two notes one beat, quavers GE; so too AF. Last note four beats. Put in accents—four in the bar; C on third and must be only two beats.

It is being played a third time; correct, quickly ink over with clef, time signature, tails to notes, bar lines. Time up: next test.

With a phrase of complicated rhythm, beating time with the other hand is the only security; it makes one such as this at once apparent:

which is a reminder that he must also watch for rests. In the test of two moving phrases, he must not waste a moment but try at once to seize both parts by dots, observing again the time, the notes on which they enter and at what points. The two parts with their note stems up and down have to be kept separate, though it is not always easy to distinguish them in the fleeting tones of the piano and so avoid regarding as the same as . What is the difference between a modulation to the dominant and one to the subdominant? One to the dominant means changing *s-f* to *s-fe* (it should be gone over many times), one to the subdominant changing *d-t,* to *d-ta,*, to get as far down on the other side of the tonic; and so right about again to return to the original key.

HARMONY

In preparing for the harmony questions, as many exercises as possible should be worked, revised, improved, and worked again, always with a very strict observance of the laws of writing in parts. It is useless protesting that the rules of the book are broken on every hand in modern music, and any candidate who writes in the style of Debussy will not be favourably received. For what is required in the examination he must respect them and acquire such facility in using them that he can accomplish the questions in the time allotted.

If a melody is given, outline in pencil the bass before anything else: if a bass, outline the melody. In doing so decide on the cadences, of which the full ones are not likely to occur oftener than every fourth bar, and figure below the chords it is proposed to use, though as other harmonies may equally well be possible it is best to regard these as tentative. Watch must be kept for any modulation indicated or implied: it too is not likely to appear earlier than the fourth bar and will generally be to the dominant or the relative major. It must not be entered too suddenly, and once quitted it should not be returned to. When the melody or bass has been sketched in, see that there are no grammatical errors between it and the given part. It will sometimes be found that an alteration will entail a change in the original conception of the harmony and, equally with anything that has to be struck out, it is very necessary to see that the alternative does not involve a grammatical overlook. This is a frequent cause of trouble when a student who knows much better is led into flagrant consecutives. The added part should be as artistic as it can be made with revision. The melody should be expansive and well away from the bass, leading to and from only one climax; the bass should be smoothly flowing with the use of inversions of chords so as to avoid the stiffness of root positions. Then draft in the harmonies lightly and, after deciding they are

correct, cover everything over in ink.   Great care has to be
taken to see that nothing is omitted in this inking process and
that the rubber over the pencil does not take away some
essential things.   The clarity of handwriting in the rudiments
questions is equally necessary here.

The main difficulty with most people lies in the choice of
chords and their relationships with other chords, and for this
it is essential to be able to hear mentally what has been written:
it should be no more necessary to play it than to read aloud a
written answer to understand its meaning.   The following,
which is frequently typical of elementary attempts, shows a
chordal sequence arising sometimes from more than an in-
ability to hear it:

and such things can be the more discouraging when the student
says he played them over and they sounded quite well.   The
chordal phrases in the text-book or in hymn tunes, which
require no great effort to memorize, must be the chief guide,
for they are grounded on the rules and are a correct and safe
procedure.   Practice in keyboard harmony is also helpful
because while less enterprising it must be more spontaneous.
The chordal changes do not generally need to be frequent:
they are indeed better slow-moving.   Plain simple harmonies
on notes not shorter than crotchets are always correct, no
matter how elaborate the melody may be.   A helpful rule is
that in triple time the first two beats often consist of one chord
which may even extend over the third beat as well, and that
in quadruple time the first two beats often consist of one
harmony and the third and fourth beats of another harmony.
But of this there are necessarily variations and exceptions.

Some general principles may act as guides to the student in
his choice of these slow-moving harmonies.   The repetition of

one on a weak part of the bar at the next accent is usually un-
satisfactory, and so is that of a bass note from the end of one
bar at the accent of the next—in either case it should be used
only at the beginning of the exercise.   If a rest appears in the
melody the same harmony should continue through the rest.
Too many full closes are to be avoided and should be inter-
spersed with weak ones: a full close with the third on the top
is weaker than one with the tonic on the top.   The decoration
of the essential notes of a melody, under which are framed the
harmonies, must receive special attention.   A melodic leap in
a bar will often suggest a chord which contains both notes.
As two quavers in the treble part ought not to be both harmonized, it will require to be decided which is the harmony
and which the passing-note, and the passing-note will continue in the same direction to a harmony note.   The same
decision must be exercised about auxiliary and other notes
which are dispensable, though it is complicated by the fact that
auxiliary ones may be approached or left by leap.   Otherwise
discords should be prepared like suspensions, but there is no
need to tie them.   The ninth and the thirteenth of the chords
so named are better kept in the top part.   An augmented or a
diminished interval has its settled resolution, and in conse-
quence the leading note should rise to the tonic.   A 6/4 chord
is temperamental and must be approached and quitted in the
correct way.

When one part only is to be added to a given one, the two
should between them leave no doubt as to the chording, which
must as with more parts be definitely and correctly fixed.
Often this test is done by being content with mere concords
that may imply faulty chordal progressions.   It is essential
that the harmonic structure should be solidly built.   Here is
an example from an actual treatment of a melody:

The chords should be successively I, III, IV, I, II, V, I, and so this would be more correct:

at the same time being stronger by its contrary motion. The lower part is the bass and subject to the rules of the bass, but it is freer to be melodic than in four parts. Passing-notes, auxiliary notes, and suspensions should be introduced, and if a touch of imitation can be devised it will add greatly to the musical interest. It is desirable to have rhythmical variety between the parts—that is, short notes at any point in one part should mean longer notes in the other. It really amounts to two parts in modern florid counterpoint.

The same is true with three or four parts. The style to be aimed at is contrapuntal, after that of Bach's chorales, in which the parts are as melodic as they can be made: the counterpoint is free and not strict, unless so requested. A good bass is essential to flowing parts, and the movement should be shared by all. Suppose, for instance, the following is a fragment of a melody set to be harmonized:

The plain harmonies it suggests are after this manner:

Passing-notes and suspensions similar to those in the melody should be introduced in so far as they break no rules—such as causing consecutives, which they may easily do—and the passage might be developed into this, in which each part has a melody of its own:

Sequences should be recognized and similarly harmonized, while they may in addition be a means of saving time. If the chromatic chords of the key are within the student's resource, their use can add wonderful colour to the harmony, and they will show that he has not been content with the simple minimum prescribed but has explored further on his own account. If a setting of words is asked for, the words must be repeated in every part and the notes which go with each syllable correctly indicated by slurs or by joined quaver strokes also slurred. Whenever possible the phrasing should be inserted, in the case of music for strings the bowing, for a real musician phrases and bows as instinctively as he punctuates a letter.

FORM

The questions on form vary with different examinations, but whatever their nature the best method of preparing for them is to keep a small note-book and enter in it a synopsis in abbreviated terms of each subject to be known. The text-book has several hundreds of pages made up of elaboration and illustration, and their essence, which is all that is wanted, can be concentrated into a dozen of note-book. It can fit into a pocket and its contents should be memorized.

The subjects generally to be noted are the sonata form of Bach and Handel, the classical sonata, the minuet and trio, the scherzo, the rondo (old and new), the fugue, and the movements of the suite. The lettering for the various forms is simple and useful and should be applied whenever possible. Binary form is AB, ternary ABA, and the essential difference between them is that the A of binary ends in a modulation while the A of ternary ends in the original key. The first section of sonata form is binary with its ending out of the key; but taking its three sections it is best regarded as a whole as ternary. Rondo form may be lettered ABACA, in which B and C are episodes in related keys. Rondo sonata form may be expressed as ABA, Development, AB, which differs from pure sonata form in the repetition of A before the development. Each form should be enforced by analysis of examples prescribed by the text-book. Some of these the candidate should consider in more detail, remarking on the use of chords, diatonic and chromatic discords, sequences in different keys, imitations, syncopations, transitions, modulations and the keys they lead to, phrases of unusual lengths and the reasons for them, the basic importance of episodes, thematic development, references to previous material, the altered treatment of the exposition in the development and in the recapitulation, the accumulating interest in a set of variations, the progressive drama in a fugue—thus furnishing himself with everything that leads to his understanding of the music and that may be pointed out for the profit of his own students. Besides, it will enable him to grasp in a few minutes the salient features of an unfamiliar movement which he may be asked to analyse and edit for performance.

Questions of this kind are allotted a restricted place, and the student must practise on what has been set in previous papers by writing out the relevant answers in small legible hand and in compact style, consisting of facts and not of sentiments, with complete and not abbreviated words, without one that is unnecessary, and making sure that they fit into the few inches of space provided.

Suppose for this purpose the following piece is given in notes only. The first thing to do is to read it over, hear it mentally, and observe its general plan, characteristic lineaments, its

[continued on pages 18–19

form and changes of key. Then read it over again quickly and number the bars. Gradually enter indications of speed, phrasing, expression, and pedalling. Then write down, as they suggest themselves, the points of analysis: they should be as far as possible, arranged in regular order.

The key is E, the form ternary—A, 1–8(2); B, 8(3)–18; A, 19–26(1); Coda, 26(2)–31.

A consists of four two-bar phrases, the first and third similar in harmony and bass, the second and fourth likewise. A special quality is imparted to the melody by accented appoggiaturas; the four cadences are plagal, imperfect, plagal, and perfect respectively and all are feminine. In the middle of the harmony is a chromatic moving part in semiquavers, which, while blurring its general effect, emphasizes some of its interior notes, and for this reason everything here will be best played half staccato. In 5 is a chromatic seventh on the tonic, and although the D is natural the key is still E.

Section B begins at 8(3) with upper semiquaver octaves on E carrying defining chords on the third and fourth of each beat, while below is a legato cello theme in the key of A, making the E's its dominant. This is repeated in A minor with fragmentary phrasing; it moves into C and at 13, by the diminished seventh, being the first inversion of the minor ninth without its root on C sharp, the supertonic of B, has a perfect cadence in that key. The phrase lengths are two of two bars and one of two and two-thirds bars. At 10 appears a double dotted quaver which is a recurring feature of the section. Now come four bars of real sequences, with basses falling in fifths to the keys of E, A, D, and G, in alternate patterns between the hands.

The return of section A would normally have been at 16, but it is delayed until 19 for the remote key of G, in which appears the first phrase as at 1 and 2 without the chromatic underpart. The second phrase, 21 and 22, is more after the form of 7 and 8 than of 3 and 4, being a reiterated cadence with full close in B, the dominant of E, to which it looks back at 15. The third phrase, again in G, is based on 5 and 6, and the last phrase, similar to 7 and 8, is in the tonic key of E which, after its long absence, beyond the hint of its dominant key in the second phrase, is emphasized by its key chord of E, second inversion, on the first beat instead of the former dominant. Between the three keys of this section the note B acts as a connecting link.

Bar 28 shows that the coda really begins at 26(1) and consists of a phrase of four beats over a bass arising from 9, and as it is repeated thrice in bars of triple time it always overlaps one beat ahead. 28(3) is 26 in the minor and the final cadence is feminine.

The piece both in harmony and modulation leans towards the flat side of the key, which, with the prevailing nature of its cadences and the unsettled rhythm of its close, suggests an easy-going indecision.

Finally, when all preparation has been made and the paper is laid before him, the candidate must, let it be repeated once more, read each question several times in order to grasp its full implications. There is only one interpretation to be put upon it, and the one and only way of supplying nothing less and nothing more than is asked must be put down at once. He should deal first with the easier and more profitable questions. He will understand that those on harmony carry more marks and take the longest time. He will see to it that he keeps sufficient margin for revision and that he is fully occupied up to the last moment. He cannot afford to waste a moment or a mark. The time allotted is just enough to do what is required, and then it is at an end.

Diplomas in Pianoforte Playing

For most diplomas in piano playing the candidate is expected to prepare scales and arpeggios, read at sight, and perform three works, of which one is in contrapuntal style, another is a classical sonata, and the third is modern romantic music. The choice from lists provided lies with the candidate. This means that he has to familiarize himself with the writing of the early eighteenth, the early nineteenth, the late nineteenth or twentieth centuries, a comprehensive scheme that covers the best of the literature of the instrument.

This part of the examination should be taken on a different day from the paper-work.

SCALES AND ARPEGGIOS

As aural tests are the foundation of harmony, so are scales and arpeggios the foundation of music. Of such importance are they that they must be practised regularly and in every variety. Scales should be done in varying rhythms, but for examination purposes groups of four are expected, and as in their preparation the time is quickened by the occasional metronome the groups will become eights, maintaining an even legato tone from finger action without arm weight as the hands flit over the keys. Always must the time be strictly kept, with no rallentando or holding on at the end. The most difficult points are the lowest and topmost notes. Facility can be increased by beginning on every other note of the scale as well as the first. Similarly scales in thirds and sixths should begin at different points. A sometimes neglected form is the left hand alone starting from the top, returning of course to end where it began; another is starting with both hands at the extremes in contrary motion. Another important consideration is the changed positions of the thumbs in going from ascending to descending in the melodic minor scales of G flat and E flat. The position too of the left-hand thumb in beginning from the top of E flat harmonic minor must be remembered. Every form should be practised hands singly and together, legato, with finger and wrist staccato, softly and loudly, crescendo and diminuendo.

Scales in double octaves should be played with the hands up towards the black notes and the fingers kept in touch with the notes to be played. In legato form care must be taken of the varying distances between the thumb and the fourth and fifth fingers; the tone is produced generally by exertion of the hand, and the two notes must be of equal strength. Staccato octaves are done by wrist movement. The simplest way of memorizing the fingering of scales in double thirds is to note where the fifth finger is in each hand, as it appears only once within the octave. It can be expressed in this very concise manner:

R.H. sharp scales to 5 sharps have 5 on the 5th degree.

R.H. flat scales to 6 flats have 5 on G.

L.H. sharp scales to 6 sharps have 5 on A.

L.H. flat scales to 5 flats have 5 on the 6th degree.

Double sixths are seldom required, but a similar synopsis round the single appearances of the middle fingers in the octave can easily be found from a scale book.

Arpeggios in their corresponding variety will be learned at first by playing them with their inversions in their plain chordal forms, and then moving on to their broken forms in groups of four. The rule for their fingering, as well as that of scales, when they begin on black notes, is that in the right hand the thumb will be placed on the lowest white note and in the left hand on the highest white note. The action of the thumb is the feature that requires greatest care. The dominant seventh is built on the dominant of the key, the diminished seventh on its leading note. The one difficulty with the dominant seventh is the interval of the second occurring between the seventh and the root in moving to the next octave above or below.

After all the scales and arpeggios have been mastered, the subsequent practice must be arranged with every variety both of form and of key, so that they may be entirely disconnected from each other. It is best to draw up a list of them so as to save time, such as:

1. G flat a third apart.
2. D first inversion contrary.
3. A flat harmonic minor in staccato double octaves.
4. C dominant seventh, second inversion.
5. B flat in double thirds, left hand from the top.
6. G melodic minor beginning on D, right hand only.

And so on. This develops the necessary quick thinking, for whenever each of them is named in irregular order, as it will be in the examination, it should without hesitation arise and speed its way perfectly over the keyboard. Played legato the rate should be about 176, with four notes to each stroke of the metronome, played staccato it should be about 152. But the aim for them all should be evenness rather than speed. A scale is expected to be done once, an arpeggio twice, four octaves in similar, two octaves in contrary, motion: three octaves is the limit for scales in double octaves.

SIGHT READING

Like everything else in preparation for a serious examination, sight reading is satisfactorily acquired by regular practice, but it is a more than usually pleasant exercise because it means exploring unfamiliar music with less responsibility than set pieces, while it affords one the satisfaction of evident progress and of a widening range of appreciation opening out before him. He is rapidly building up a stock of experience which will bring its rich reward. The test requires a finished performance at the correct speed and with everything of phrasing and expression. The pedal must be used.

It is better to begin with what is within one's capacity and gradually move to what is more difficult. The musical student, however, will give little time to grading. He finds the slow movements of classical sonatas generally simpler and slower than the other movements, but he cannot help turning to these also, unaware perhaps that he may be merely skimming their surface; that does not matter—he is taking one of the most potent steps in his advancement, for borne forward by the prestige of the composer's name and its reflection upon himself, he is intrigued into a romantic adventure with plenty of incident on the way. He will try everything that comes to his hand to thrill at the effects he may light upon.

He has learned for himself what is required in approaching new music. It is an exercise of the mind and of the eye together. First he must look at the key signature and the time signature, inwardly marking the beats of the bar. The key and the time he must keep steadily before him. Then by looking over the piece he will get an idea of its style and prevailing rhythm, the changes of signatures that may occur, the passages with shorter notes which may dictate the speed, the general line of expression. He should look at the keyboard as little as may be necessary; the majority of people spend far too much time losing the place on the page to find a note actually

below a hand and then recovering the place again. The
student must make a habit of feeling between the black and
white keys and by exchanging a finger on a note find another
outside the immediate reach of an octave. Only by doing so
are those without sight able to play at all. For instance, in
this:

there is no need to look down to find the low D: the high D
gives the position of the octave below it and by exchanging the
thumb for the fifth finger over that note, without playing it,
the fifth finger automatically gets the required note another
octave lower:

With practice this can be acquired quickly so as not to disturb
the rhythm. It will greatly facilitate reading at sight.

It will also do something scarcely less important—it will
enable the player to keep his head still. Even when he is
looking for a note he seldom requires to move his head. If he
wears spectacles, he will find their outer rims dislocating the
lines of the stave and of the keyboard and by moving his head
the dislocation will vary accordingly; with bifocal lenses it will
be doubled. He should therefore have plain reading spectacles which when worn form one round glass. His head
should be in such position that the top of the music and the
keyboard are within the range of the glass, and so he will move
only his eyes if he should have to look for a note. Thus will he
always be on the spot.

As he now tries over the piece, it is more important to play
correctly than up to speed, and if he makes a mistake he should
go on and not stop to put it right. He must look ahead.
Knowing as he does the chords of the key and how especially

the primary ones form the basis of the music, he regards it as a series of harmonies. He has to recognize broken chords in their unbroken forms, how they generally move to a pattern and in their slow progress give him time to grasp them. These harmonies will show any unessential notes added to them and also to the melody; the melody he will look upon as a series of ascending and descending climaxes which he will naturally express with clear phrasing. His hold of the key will enable him to meet the accidentals, but still better, especially in contrapuntal music in long bars, will be his listening with a harmonic sense so that he can know without looking back whether accidentals are still effective. This will carry him safely through recurring figures with chromatic unessential notes. His feeling for a cadence, for instance, should render it impossible for him to overlook what must be the continuing sharp influences in such a passage as this:

Should he chance to neglect them and not be shocked, he has ceased to listen. When he has finished the piece, he should try it again and see how much more he can put into it.

Another profitable form of practice is to be found in piano-duet playing, with its discipline of partnership, strict time, and continuity. It has a vast library of music whose effectiveness is twice what one contributes to it. All that is required is a willing partner. Opportunity too should be sought of playing accompaniments for a reliable instrumentalist or singer or choir, which will likewise extend the student's repertoire of other types of music. For the purposes of sight reading, however, the richest material is to be found in Bach. The inventions, the suites, the partitas are there to provide beautiful thoughts with every technical device. Nearly every bar is different and must be carefully watched : nothing can be taken for granted. The '48,' with a prelude and fugue for each day, will last forty-eight days, and they will build up enough experience and facility for whatever may be presented at any examination.

TECHNIQUE AND INTERPRETATION

The candidate must study the different kinds of touch which produce the various styles of playing, such as velocity, brillante, and cantabile. Touch means movement. It is of three kinds : (1) finger action only, (2) hand and finger but not used at the same time, and without the arm, (3) arm weight added to the other two, with again only one moving and the touch named after the part which moves. For the purpose of piano playing each finger has two sets of muscles, one to lower the note, the other to let it rise, and if both are used together the result is stiffness. Its action has strong influence on the tone and this is exerted during the downward movement of the key, not before or after. The key must not be hit, nor should strength or effort be wasted in holding it down, for no further influence on the tone is possible. The natural condition is muscular freedom. For quick passages and ornaments finger touch is employed, the tips of the fingers gliding along at the required speed, but sounding every note. Brilliance is acquired by depressing the keys rapidly and adding to velocity the resting weight from the lower part of the arm.

For legato playing finger touch is used, for quick chords hand touch, for slower chords arm touch. As an antidote to stiffness correct rotary adjustment is essential. The majority of technical faults are due to too much rotary exertion towards the thumb, which weakens the other fingers. The omission of this exertion when not required produces free action.

The different lengths of notes are shown in the variations of legato and staccato, and they have an important part in interpretation. When we play a note, we have to decide the amount of tone, its quality, when it is to be played and when it is to cease. Tone length and tone quality are two different things: in the length of tone we are concerned with tone gradation, but in the quality of tone with tone colour. Legato playing is dependent on the differences of amount and quality of the sounds, with no silence between them. Rarely have two successive notes the same tone amount, and cantabile effects on the piano with its diminishing tone can never be more than a makeshift. The legato effect is obtained by releasing the weight of the whole arm and guiding it behind the selective action of the fingers. As each key is depressed the climax must be kept in view. A crescendo and a diminuendo must be built up, each note in proportion to the previous one. There ought to be no jerkiness, and greater security in this is acquired by every care for the fingering, which may accord with that for scales or arpeggios, for sequence formulae or for groups, so that the finger groups are prompted by the note groups. It may preserve the rhythm, for which the tempo has to be considered. For the legato of a melody any effective fingering is correct, from changing on a note to sliding from a black to a white note. In fast time the turn of the thumb should be used as little as possible.

Staccato, for which the finger, the hand, the arm may be employed, begins and ends on the surface of the key, and it may differ from that of other keys in the same phrase: it may have to be added though not indicated. For detached cantabile more arm weight is necessary. Short notes are generally played softer than long ones. In two-note phrases there is hand action, finger action, then release. The variations of time in a phrase mean rubato and are the slowing or quickening of beats for some important point dictated by the music. They do not alter the length of time a phrase occupies; their changes are very slight, for if overdone the phrase becomes shapeless. Ideas of colour are founded on the orchestra, and we must be able to recognize the tones of the various instruments and understand their characteristic uses. This brings imagination into interpretation.

The artistic influence of the right-foot pedal should be considered from the beginning. Mistakenly called the 'loud' pedal, its purpose is by removing the dampers to hold on notes beyond the reach of the hands, to enrich their tone by allowing the other strings to vibrate in sympathy with them, and to release them at the required moment. There are different ways of employing the pedal. With legato chords it should be depressed after each one and lifted before the next one is played: this is known as 'harmonic pedalling.' In 'half-pedalling,' as in arpeggios with changing harmonies above, it is allowed half up, just enough to extinguish the upper tones and allow the bass notes with their thicker strings to continue sounding. In 'half-damping,' as in running passages, the pedal is not completely depressed and the dampers do not come entirely away from the strings but remain partially in contact with them. In half-pedalling it is the length of time the dampers stay on the strings that matters: in half-damping it is the distance they are from the strings which gives it its special effect of resonance. The left-foot pedal, indicated by 'una corda,' is simply held down until it is due to rise with the words 'tre corde.' An inspection of the inside of the piano will reveal how the two pedals act, how the dampers rest on the strings and are lifted off them by the action of the right foot, how the top strings with their fragile tone do not require dampers, that the pedal has to be renewed more frequently in the lower half of the keyboard than the upper; that with the left-foot pedal the keyboard of a grand moves slightly to the right, so that the hammers may strike a limited number of strings, or that on an upright a piece of felt is raised between the hammers and strings to produce softer tone. The fact remains that the fingers can produce equally soft tone independently of this pedal, even with the 'loud' pedal down.

THE PRELUDE AND FUGUE

In selecting the contrapuntal piece of music, such as a prelude and fugue, the student will be wise, other things being equal, to avoid what is easier and more popular and to decide on what is bright rather than serious, for it will hold his interest and keep up his spirits better during his weeks of preparation. And, what is given too little thought, it will have a more favourable effect on the examiners, whose lot requires all the alleviation that may be afforded it.

The main source for such a piece is Bach's 48 Preludes and Fugues, but if there is the novelty of an alternative it should be carefully considered. In any case it provides an admirable training in method and technique. Further profit is to be gained from the fact that Bach wrote only the notes of his music and left everything else to the taste of the artist, a compliment which adds to his responsibilities. As the sustaining pedal was unknown, every note is intended to be held on by the finger for its full value until it moves on to the next one, and this may be complicated by the necessity of changing the finger for another during the length of the note. A rest is to receive as much attention and, as the parts mount in number, it may be specially important in lightening the texture of the harmony. Control must be contrived by avoiding any break in a part to make it perfectly clear in its movement. For this purpose the tone has to be arranged so that

does not sound as

This applies equally when a part enters above or below one already moving, as in the same prelude, 24 of the '48':

where the C sharp must be shown by accent to be the first note of the top part, arising from the minim rest and not from the B of the part below.   Arpeggios, as in Preludes 3, 6, and 39, with accents at the top, the middle, and the foot respectively, should all be taken at first as unbroken chords; in addition to simplifying the practice of the moving harmonies this gives a bird's-eye view of their purpose.   There is not much in Bach of a hand having to change its position suddenly for another: when it occurs, each position may be simple enough, but the difficulty lies in making the sudden change accurately, and that must be examined and gone over slowly until it is secure. Take this left-hand phrase, for instance, from Fugue 3 (the key of which should cause no more trouble than any other):

The passage is in sequence and is best taken as chords:

giving special care to the leap in the first half of the sequence figure and to the second leap to the next sequence: it does not matter for the purpose that the accents are displaced; the leaps are the essential things. The passage might be still more clearly epitomized thus:

The phrasing and expression arise naturally from the spirit of the music. Generally speaking, even where an editor's long slurs appear in the copy—those of Czerny, for a bad instance, in the Peters edition—the phrasing consists of little groups of a few notes to give the argument active life. In Bach a phrase often begins on a weak point of the bar and ends on a normal accent, so that in playing it we give the first note a slight emphasis and make the last a light staccato, with the result that as the accent is displaced the effect is that of syncopation. In sequences, as at the end of Prelude 15 where they descend through a whole octave, and in the innumerable passages which reappear imitated or inverted, the phrasing should be uniform, though the fingering need not be. A series of semi-quavers followed by quavers will usually require the quavers to be staccato so as to clarify the moving parts elsewhere. In Preludes 14, 15, and 21, where staccato is an intrinsic feature, many students tend to reduce the feeling of jerkiness it causes; but this is to be resisted and the staccato must be consistently maintained.

In approaching the fugue the same principles of study equally apply. Whatever the nature of the prelude the fugue is always polyphonic and must have continuity in its flow of parts. This brings its own problems, and attention has to be specially concentrated on the points that give trouble. The

phrasing of the subject is of the first importance and is generally prompted by its characteristic vitality or by some feature
such as a rest or a sequence, as in these:

These phrasings ought to prevail with every appearance of the
subjects and answers, which when possible should be slightly
emphasized.   But additional drollery may be imparted to
them by slight variations when, for instance, they enter in a
minor key; as in the first example, slight staccato for the romp
of both sequential groups, and in the second example a ten-
dency to slur the first two and the third and fourth notes.   The
same varied consistency should apply also to the episodes.   It
is personal touches of this kind which help to lend distinction
to a performance.   The interest of a fugue is cumulative from
the development of the subject and its answer as they enter
with new meanings in a carefully considered key system, and
it lies in the hands of the player to raise the humour and
excitement until he gathers the parts together to their cadential
conclusion, whether in a climax of tone, a shading off over a
long held bass, or in a note of seriousness with a favourite re-
entry and final word from the tenor.

Both prelude and fugue have definite forms and these should
be studied in such works as Stewart Macpherson's and Iliffe's
Analysis of the '48.'   Every detail should be noted and understood: the economy manifested by the composer in building
the two movements on short phrases or even fragments of
them, the key relationships, the reality or tonality of the fugue,
for what voices, the distances between their entries, the
countersubject, the strettos, the material on which the episodes
are   framed   and   their   lengths,   anything   in   the   way   of

augmentation, diminution, double or triple counterpoint, the
limitations imposed by the contemporary keyboard and its
lack of sustaining pedal, any features involving unusual
harmonies, the tierce-de-Picardie at the end.   The outlines of
the composer's life and times are helpful towards a better
understanding of his style, while the profit to be derived from
careful study of this treasury of his should be diagnosed so as
to support the contention that every aspect of the technique of
piano playing is to be found in it.

If we open the first book of the '48' at the thematic index,
we see that the preludes with their fugues, major and minor,
proceed up each degree of the chromatic scale, the majors the
odd numbers, the minors the even.   The scale is completed by
the twenty-four pieces of the book, and it is explored further by
another set on the same principle in the second book.

Turning over again we come upon the well-known prelude
in C, a series of quiet broken chords such as Bach at the end of
a heavy day might improvise before going off to rest.   The
arpeggios move to a pattern, each bar consisting of one chord
done twice, the repetition being an echo of the first; so slowly do
the harmonies move, and the pedal can be used for every bar:

The chords should be gone over in their plain forms:

not only to perceive their simple progress but to see their
rhythm with its rise and fall, in which lie such phrasing and

expression as are possible.   Only at the third last bar is the pattern given up to broaden out the final cadence.   In the second last bar it looks as though Bach intended a legatissimo effect, to which he was partial, whereby the D on the third beat, though only a semiquaver, may be held on and made to arrive on the C of the last bar:

Otherwise he would have chosen that the low semiquaver D should rise to E as the top of the closing chord, which indeed he actually did at the very same place in the second prelude immediately following.

The fugue is in four parts, and while the subject appears in the treble stave it must be played by the left hand as the answer enters above it in the second bar.   Their phrasing may be considered thus:

and will generally be maintained with each entry.   The question arises, where does the subject end? and the reply is to be found in the so-called 'answer,' which copies the subject a fifth higher as far as B, the first note of bar 4: this shows the subject ends with the corresponding E, as above.   And as the answer is an exact transposition of the subject, the fugue is said to be real.   It will be observed also that while the subject with its one and a half bars starts off the first beat of the bar, the answer does so off the third, that as they proceed they enter variously off all four beats, giving the impression that the time is two in the bar rather than four.   The texture of the writing is very rich as the parts build up many bars of sixteen semi-quavers of complicated movement. In the midst of this they provide exciting examples of stretto, for which purpose the composer chose the subject: there are no fewer than six of them, three with all four parts taking their share. They enter one beat, two, three, or four beats apart and at almost every interval above or below, and they are so preoccupied with these devices that they forget to allow room for a single episode. The subject is constantly present and as it moves by step there is scarcely any chance for the pedal here. The last four bars are grounded upon a single bass C, of which little will be left when the right hand at last mounts up on wings to its final chord: on Bach's faint instrument nothing whatever of it can have remained.

And so on does the work proceed. There is something in it to meet every mood and every taste. The student having made his choice, he should first of all go over the two numbers with both hands so as to get a general impression of them. After that, during the next few weeks, it is essential to take them with each hand separately in slow but strict time, watching particularly where scales are divided between the hands or parts are shared by them, or when left-hand notes are written in the upper stave, right-hand ones in the lower. These are characteristic features of the music of the period. Where the fingering indicated proves inconvenient, it should be altered to what is more suitable and with the rest followed implicitly. In the meantime, as the part for each hand is becoming better known, the phrasing will be suggesting itself, and as may be deemed necessary should be inserted and maintained consistently throughout. Then when all is assured the two hands may be united, slowly at first and with every care that the time is regular with frequent discipline from the metronome at a reduced rate. Gradually will the speed be worked up to what is appropriate to the mood of the music: it will be an advantage indeed to increase it to a still higher speed to make the proper one simpler. Ornaments, which are omitted until the

D

framework is sure, must on no account disturb the rhythm but, as in writing them out in the rudiments paper, fit into the lengths of the notes which carry them.   Long trills, whether for right or left hand, as in Preludes 11 and 16, are to be evenly played and given special attention as to their endings.   Advantage has to be taken of such resource as is offered by the pedal of a modern piano, and, keeping the essential matters in view, its use should be very carefully calculated : at most points it will be only momentary, or half-pedalling, for though the harmonies may move slowly there are likely to be auxiliary and other notes, such as those from ornaments, which are foreign to them and not intended to be retained ; but when the chording is clear the pedal can greatly enrich the effect.   This is equally true of the fugue ; but here the opportunity for the pedal is still more limited as it is more necessary that nothing should be allowed to overcast the balance of tone and the movement of the parts.   Now any possible rallentando should be added, such as in the prelude a very slight one at a full or half close rounding off a section, and one at the final cadence— still only slight for the fugue is to follow.   The rallentando at the end of the fugue will have to be devised after much experiment.

It is important to remember that to regard these miniatures as though they are of archaic interest and need only be mechanical in their effect is not sufficient.   Bach's music calls for more than its being unfolded accurately and in time.   Its spirit must be absorbed and adequately expressed, and for that experience and intelligence are required.   He meant every note of it ; he wrote only when he had something to say, and such was the urgency of his message that, with no manuscript paper—for it was unknown—and having to draw his own staves, he repeatedly revised and rewrote it to its perfection.   It is chamber music for a select circle, revealing to us some of the personal touches they knew so well—the varying mood, the thoughtfulness and the gaiety, the accomplished playing, above all the goodness of his character.   Such pieces as these did he dispense to them behind the closed door. Even now they make us feel we have been admitted to a step on the threshold, enabling us to overhear him at his clavi-chord, and how full of generous fancy they are as they come through to us!

These then are among the pages prescribed by a wise fore-sight for the examination. They are with a thousand other works as real to-day as when they came forth from the mind of him of whom it has been said that music owes to him almost as great a debt as Christianity owes to its founder. And so surely it should always be an occasion when we play them.

THE SONATA

The centre of the practical examination lies in the sonata, which consists of three or four movements, affords wider scope for interpretation in its variety of mood, and uses all the resources of the modern piano. It is the chief test in playing, and the choice of the work has an important bearing on the examiners' impression of the candidate. It is unwise to take one because it presents fewer difficulties than others: it should rather be one that entails solid preparation and suits his particular powers of technique and interpretation. If he is not confident in fluent passage work, he will decide against most of Mozart's, for despite their appearance they are not easy from their lightness of texture, with scales and arpeggios exposed to the open and little to support them; nothing but clean, confident playing will do. If he has a small hand he had better avoid one with running octaves, such as Beethoven's op. 54. There are plenty of others offering a choice, though none of Beethoven's is technically simple except the two of op. 49 and op. 79, and even they call for all the artistry one has at command.

With these works we enter a different world. The scope of the music has broadened out and made possible a new instrument and new standards of playing. Compared with the harpsichord, the piano allows for every balance of tone and refinement of phrasing, the pedal sustains harmonies while the hands sweep the limits of the extended keyboard, and the easier action allows of greater speed. Mozart and Beethoven were themselves masters of an instrument with a lighter touch and softer tone than we know, and their music provides opportunities not only for brilliance of technique but for every shade of feeling and expression. The writing is thinner and seldom polyphonic while the movements have taken new forms which are not stereotyped but vary with the needs of the composer. With Beethoven in particular they had to be free to cope with the more liberal ideas and aspirations of the new century.

These forms have a strong influence on our interpretation of them. We must differentiate between them; we must distinguish the subjects and their development and see that the sections are collateral, such as the high moment, often so subtly contrived, leading into the return and a maturer aspect of the first subject in the fresh light that has just been shed upon it. All the movements have to be integrated to make the whole work one complete unity. It is essential, therefore, to study the forms of Beethoven's various sonatas under the guidance of such a book as Harding's *Analysis of Form*. This will help us not only in our playing of them but also to perceive that the composer had a purpose in every bar and in every change of key, and that his repetitions were due not to his having nothing new to write but to the claims of the forms which we ourselves have to acknowledge to be inherent in them.

The methods of studying a sonata are the same as for everything else, slow practice of hands singly with due care for fingering and phrasing. As in Bach, the left hand must be as efficient as the right. When the hands are confidently united, there is no need to go through a whole movement each time: more good is derived by concentrating on awkward points and going over them and over them until they are thoroughly mastered. The movements are taken concurrently.

What many students lack in looking into the details of such a work is a set of principles with which to meet difficulties and analyse them to their simplification and solution. In addition, with such principles they can save a great amount of time and trouble. There are two main circumstances from which they may be acquired. One lies in the physical conditions entailed in the act of playing. Two hands and two arms have their special mechanisms and the piano has its own, all of which have to be carefully considered towards achieving a good performance. The actions of the fingers, of the forearm, and of the arm will all affect the touch and the phrasing and the expression. But the student has particularly to consider the capabilities and restrictions of his own two hands. Unsuitable fingering can make it impossible for him to render a certain passage: if he cannot, for instance, change fingers on legato octaves he will have to keep to a uniform fingering. To him rapid four-note chords may provide their individual problem of getting clearly the two middle notes. Right-hand chords in the bass and left-hand ones in the treble, such as appear in the Scherzo of op. 28:

will mean that his fingers are at an angle to the line of the keys, and they call for very watchful care. So do leaps of a tenth:

One is apt to be lulled from the facts by the circumstance that all tenths look the same in print.   But they have their decided differences.   Each must be taken by the hand at full stretch: the little extra required is what creates the difficulty.   E to G' has a right-hand movement along the horizontal plane of the keyboard; compared with this, E flat to G' has actually a triple deviation from the plane as the thumb moves outwards, upwards, and to the left to get E flat; E to G' sharp has a similar triple movement, but by the fifth finger at the opposite side of the hand.   Again, F to A' and F to A' flat are both the same distance apart as radii of a circle with the thumb at the centre, but lower these notes a semitone, E to G' sharp and E to G', and they are not the radii of any circle.   Furthermore, E to G' and G to B', while not the same musical interval, are the same physical interval and entail the same amount of movement. G flat to B flat has a little problem of its own from the narrowness of the keys.

The other circumstance, which helps us to a different set of principles, lies in the limitations under which the composer works.   He cannot write simply what he likes.   If he wishes his music to be performed and memorized, and incidentally be in demand at the publishers, he must conform to certain normal formulae arising from decoration of a plain harmonic background, which have a certain consistency in their activity and have the performer in view so as to help him, and it is the performer's duty to himself to find these formulae.

For instance, in the trio of op. 2, no. 1, he should notice for himself that after four bars the left hand repeats a version of the right hand, that something similar happens beyond the double bar, and that the last eight bars are with very slight changes the same as the first eight.   Of the changes he must make special note.   Similarly, in the Scherzo of op. 26, eight bars of the right hand are repeated in the left with two single notes in sequence altered for one and the same reason.   A more complete case appears near the end of op. 90, where the two hands flit about in contrary motion with similar figures. But there is more to it than that.   By looking into it the student should observe that the figures are not only similar but the same—one figure of two bars, that the left hand leads the way and the right sets off with the same figure a bar later when the other is half way, that this is done three times, and once more the half of it by the left:

There are thus only two bars to practise and they can be done by both hands together two octaves apart.

As with Bach, broken chords and octaves are, where possible, best practised as unbroken ones; they are to be found in every sonata, but particularly in the first, in the finale of op. 28, and in two movements of the 'Moonlight'; the first movement of the 'Moonlight' can by this means be memorized within an hour. But now with Beethoven's broken chords there is much more of suddenly darting to a new position of the hand, a novelty which the sustaining pedal made possible. His op. 27, no. 1, offers an example in this:

which at first with the correct fingering should be treated as:

But that of itself does not solve the situation. Each chord is simple enough, but the right hand leaps from 1 to 2, 3 to 4, 5 to 6, in each case to something different—in the last, up one degree short of two octaves—and the left hand also from 5 to 6 to the same chord with different fingering. These leaps and the need that they should be cleanly done are the difficulties of the passage and must be gone over many times.

At the end of the same movement is to be found this:

The chief concern here lies in the left-hand octave arpeggios of plain chords with varying distances at two points, between the two lower notes and between the lowest and the first of the next chord. These cannot be simplified and must be practised as they are, slowly with the octave distance between thumb

and fifth finger strictly immovable, and to increase speed the
hand should be up the white notes towards the blacks and play
the A flat and B flat at the outer ends of their notes, so that it
may move in as near a straight line as possible.   Then can be
added the right hand with its plain chords in one place, until
ultimately as written with their second and third notes the
same as the first two of the left, but in the opposite direction,
and its legato formation coming between the regular staccato
of the left.   As the right offers no difficulty it should be practised without looking at it, for the eyes have to be reserved
exclusively for the left.   The whole movement is to be played
at high speed, and so these two passages from it with their
particular obstacles have to be memorized.

Another form of arpeggio, which cannot be reduced to
chords but can be simplified towards memorizing it, and
therefore playing it, is to be seen in the second movement of
op. 78:

A glance shows that the second of each couple of notes belongs
to the chord and the first one is an appoggiatura a semitone
below.   The pattern of repetition is not consistently followed,
and it has to be regarded in this way:

But that is only partially helpful. The essential thing in playing the passage is to manage the leaps, that is to the appoggiaturas, and the second notes will come automatically. The appoggiaturas, it is to be noticed, are all white notes, forming the chord of C, and so if they be taken with their companion notes in the key of C they become this in principle:

and this is the best way to get up the passage. It is not so much the leaps of an arpeggio as those of two arpeggios combined. Now there are three features here needing special attention. One is that the second of the four combinations differs from the others in having two white notes instead of a white and a black; another is that in going from G to C' the hand moves a fourth instead of a third like the other two; and the last feature is that the left hand, compared with the right, becomes awkwardly uncomfortable as it rises towards the top at an increasing angle of arm position. Keeping these points in view the student must go over (b) many times, hands singly and together, two, three octaves up and down. Then he turns to the pattern of (a), continuing to omit the six sharps and be in the key of C. This must be repeated until it is completely familiar, making sure that, as in Beethoven's page, while the right hand leads the way the left has the rhythmical accents, and then last of all with the two notes played separately. In this way the passage can be got up in half the time. Later in the movement two similar flights have greater force with the left hand beginning on the first beats of the bars, and they have similarly to be approached by the chords formed by the appoggiaturas. These passages are better without pedal.

A more elaborate example of broken chords is to be found in a brilliant section in only two parts on the last page of op. 28:

The left hand, again in octaves, has the theme with which it opened the movement in single notes, and in the continually active right hand it is to be observed that the first four notes of each bar form a turn, the first an under one, the others upper ones. These all spin around the second note, and so to memorize the passage, as must certainly be done, it can be reduced to this simple formula:

These four bars are immediately repeated with the under turn now made an upper one and the last G made F so as to repeat bars 3 and 4 twice more and bar 4 once again. Here as before it is essential that the right-hand part, with its important fingering and no phrasing, should become so familiar that one is free to look exclusively at the left, where all the dangers lie.

Now Beethoven was perfectly capable of writing here another brilliant page, full of elaborations in haphazard order and leading nowhere in particular. But it would have been left on his hands to play it himself: no one else would take the trouble to memorize it because there would be no principle behind it. What we have in the sonata, therefore, is intentionally based on the opening melody below and the first bar above which gives a clue to all the others, so that we can anticipate what they will be, and the rest consists of methodical repetition. These are the principles of the passage; they have been put there to give relevance to the coda of the movement and as aids to the player. The page may be beyond his power at the prescribed speed, but it is well within his power to find them as a guide to centralizing his practice of it.

Such are some of the means towards the technical accomplishment of these works, and the principles underlying them will be guides for others. But beyond them, and where they ultimately lead, is the inner meaning behind the notation. That takes longer to come. And yet, apart from the variety of interpretation which will distinguish all thoughtful performances and give each its own individuality, Beethoven's music ought to be played as he has indicated. He was careful to express what he wanted and liberties with it are taken at the cost of the player. It must never be sentimentalized: his spirited moods must be bold and vigorous, his softer ones only quieter for they are still those of a brave man dealing with other aspects of expression. Of whatever kind they may be, they can be adequately interpreted at last after acquiring long familiarity with his music and complete command of the keyboard.

Let me suppose that I am thinking of being a candidate for a diploma requiring three works, and that I am selecting the sonata. One without running passages and octaves would suit well, though none of these works is free of them altogether, and I consider Beethoven's fifth number, op. 10, no. 1, in C minor, with which I am, of course, already familiar. It is somewhat hackneyed, but it is not easy, and I would have to play it after the most fastidious preparation to impress examiners who hear it so frequently. It extends to fourteen pages and has only three movements: one with four would be a better offering. The key, while it lasts, less than a third of the whole work, is a little sombre and the outer movements are hectic. But it is brilliant, and if I take it I would be wise to have the Bach number and also the third one in a quieter contrast of major keys. I must think, too, of the key relationships of the three works: it would not be good to have them in C major, C minor, and C major respectively, which would soon become tiring. I must consider further a variety of sentiment, for I have to form the programme of a short well-chosen recital. As it is included in the list, I decide on this sonata and arrange the others around it.

I search the library for references to it. It was written in Vienna round about the composer's twenty-seventh year. When it and its two companion sonatas of op. 10 were published, Closson says, they were regarded 'as an accumulation of ideas arranged in an odd manner' and 'as artificial obscurities.' An early book on the sonatas by Elterlein does not provide much beyond expressing the opinion that the first two movements reflect Mozart and the third and most original shows the composer's own individuality breaking through. Taylor in his *Technique and Expression in Pianoforte Playing* mentions the sonata twice, and in his primer he makes several points about the ornaments: on the other hand Dannreuther in his *Ornamentation* has nothing on them. Prout in his *Applied Forms* analyses the slow movement and Reddie speaks of one of its rhapsodical phrases. Henry Fisher in his *Mentor* twice refers to the form. Tovey in his *Encyclopaedia Britannica* article on 'Rhythm' makes an interesting allusion to an anacrusis in the first page of the sonata, while his unfinished monograph on the composer devotes a page to it. I keep beside me for frequent reference his *Companion* to the sonatas and his notes to his edition of them. Eric Blom's *Beethoven's Sonatas Discussed* treats of the form, and Harding, too, is at hand with his *Analysis*. I have numbered the bars throughout in fives.

I set about solving some of the technical dangers—at the very beginning the arpeggios in the first line, which I take first as chords with their correct fingering but without the phrasing:

and go over them until I can play them quickly. Now I try them as written:

with special care to observe their acute rhythm and not as though they were triplets: that would ruin their effect. They crescendo up to the two top notes, which are to be emphatically staccatissimo. At bar 13 in some editions the tie between the low G of the arpeggio and the low dotted crotchet is omitted: it should be inserted here and at bar 180. After a diminuendo, 21 comes in with great emphasis and an awkward leap in the right hand, which does not appear again but must be gone over several times:

and at 28 and 29 there are tenths the same distance apart, in watching which one is apt to overlook the left hand, but it must be played loudly and with wrist staccato:

This is a very impatient Beethoven, but how smiling in the following episode as he smoothly descends by three phrases in sequence through A flat, F minor, and D flat and continues down to the chord and the key of B flat by a subtle process involving two rich harmonies, one of the German sixth at 45 (all three forms of the augmented sixth appear in the one brief space) and what is potentially the chord of D major at 47, both remarkable things on which I must linger—the rhythm can stand still for the moment! The chord of B flat, with its root held on as a pedal note, turns out to be the dominant chord of E flat, an amusing surprise to prepare for the key of the second subject. I must write out the ornamental turn at 61, which is to be brought in not as written but at the end of 60, and the trill at 75, and practise them singly so that they fit in with the left hand and do not disturb its quaver activity. Then come the impatient arpeggios and staccato punctuations again, until at 90 to 92 the changing fingers on repeated notes:

which I have to go carefully over and get up to time with the rest. Much of the exposition goes well enough, and I concentrate specially on the opening arpeggios in their various forms, on the ornaments, and on the changing fingers at 90—I have them from memory and can go through them at odd minutes without opening the score—until it is all moving along at the same speed, my speed for the present.

This is the substance of the whole movement. At 116 and 117 appear again two tenths which require more care than the former ones because of the black note—it is inclined to disturb the other tenth, so over both many times. I must write out the different kind of turn at 134, and attend to the bass from 142 sliding down into the depths through sixteen bars, in contrast with the broken fragments above. After this are four bars of panting staccato phrases:

and at their immediate repetition, which ought not to be played the same way, I want to make them less staccato, by drawing the fingers inwards, as they soften with a slight rallentando to the return of the opening crash. So now comes the recapitulation, and in comparing it with the opening I notice that the first twenty-one bars are repeated exactly as before, but the full chord of 22 is reduced to plain octaves and the passage from there to 30 is omitted. These details will help me to memorize the movement. The episode begins a tone lower, in the key of G flat, repeats the first phrase an octave above, and with certain changes contrives to finish a tone higher on the chord of C, the dominant of F minor, a strange key. And the second subject surprisingly enters in the major (I must keep this in mind for possible mention at the examination), and then at last it is repeated in the tonic minor in right-hand octaves followed by arpeggios instead of the former scales. The rest is as before transposed into C minor. It is evidently in sonata form and this is confirmed by the books.

In the slow movement, in modified sonata form without development, I had better count by quavers and omit the ornaments. At bar 3 the bass A and top D must be sustained for their values, and at 5 and 6 there are double dots—he wants these, but the demisemiquavers must not be too short. At 8 the awkward note values on the third time of going over are still not right; at 9 and 11 the bass notes are to be held on. At 17, 19, and 21 the arpeggios come fairly smartly down with forcible jabs on the lowest notes, 21 with fewer notes a little slower, and the syncopated phrasing at 22 and 23 is to be precisely expressed. Bar 28 is the chief difficulty and will require a lot of practice:

for the notes are quite short in uneven groups, but the rising part is noticeably in figures of three notes separated by the intervals of the dominant seventh chord omitting the root—it is at once evident why he omits it; similarly with 30, a third higher, and they must be done very lightly as a purposeful flourish so that the rhythm of the left hand continues more or less even from the bars before and into those that follow. When these figures reappear in the key of the movement, 28 is slightly changed and 30 is curtailed. There are thus four of these phrases to occupy me for some weeks. How emphatic is the breathless crescendo from 31 with its rests and short notes, and then its repetition in triplets with an appoggiatura a semitone below each crotchet beat! The return to the opening has many little alterations and additions which need care—every detail must be scrupulously attended to. Then I go back and consider the ornaments, which will generally be slower than usual and may vary in rhythm to fit the mood; some of them are complicated by notes being held below in the

E

same hand, and 41 and 93 will need some attention.   As elsewhere, some of these things may come off successfully a dozen times and then break down on the thirteenth, showing they are not yet mastered.   They may require fifty times.

The final movement, rather ominously marked 'Prestissimo,' must be taken slowly that I may become familiar with the changing of fingers on repeated notes and the special phrasing at the very beginning, ending on an emphatic first beat:

Bars 7 and 8 are also to be gone over many times so as to go freely with the fingering:

The chief point lies in the rising arpeggio being not the dominant seventh but the diminished seventh with its normal fingering of the thumb of the right hand on B natural, that of the left on F, all played with finger staccato.   The fastest parts of the movement are those in semiquavers, which will be the test in prestissimo, but it is to be noted that in their appearance at 13 to 17, 14 is the same as 13 down an octave, the first half of 15 is the same as in both down a further octave, and the rest are chordal arpeggios.   That simplifies the outlook very considerably and makes it easy to memorize.   It is further noticeable it is to be legato in contrast with the left hand, and that although it is descending it increases in tone to a fortissimo climax on the chord of G major, the dominant. How diverting now to step in at once on staccato tiptoe in the key of E flat! Here is a Beethoven joke, and I must try to put into it the sparkle with which he wrote it. Semiquavers reappear at 29, until at 35 and 36 there are four notes against three, and looking forward I see them recur at 93 and 94. These are best overcome by doing them many times in each hand until they become automatic. The sudden leaps at the beginnings of 38 and 39, 41 and 42, comfortable enough at the present speed, must repeatedly be gone over for prestissimo when it comes. Bar 42 has the same gorgeous German sixth as in the first movement but now with full value of time and tone, and at 44 and 45 the right hand consists of two little phrases of which one is the inversion of the other, a favourite effect of the composer's appearing in the Scherzo of op. 2, no. 3, the first movement of op. 13, and the finale of op. 27, no. 1.

As at the same place in the first movement, the repetition of the exposition will not be wanted, and I must be careful to enter with the following left-hand phrase exactly on the spot. It is essential to observe here that in the right hand the four-note groups all begin with an appoggiatura a semitone below the following note, which with the other two forms a chord. The passing of the right hand over the left, where the composer hammers out his crossness, must be done by the hands together and in time, as also at the end but in a different frame. The first seventeen bars are now repeated, but there is a significant alteration of 11 and 12 at 69 and 70 to right-hand semiquavers in what turns out to be the chromatic scale from B natural to high C, the first group being a quintuplet:

The chief point here is to make sure of the accents on the B natural and the E natural—to be repeated many times with the left hand. At 99 some people assume that the A's are natural, as in the previous bar and from the phrase's earlier appearance at 41; both notes are, of course, flat. The long ritardando from 108 must not be overdone. At 114 the composer is in two minds as to what to do: 115 is one of those moments he is fond of introducing to suggest he thinks of turning elsewhere, and the arpeggio is to be played tentatively with a slight rallentando as it rises to be adagio at the top. But it comes to nothing, and with a crash the tonic chord is swept up at full speed, to soften to the major and sink to a final low murmur, the end of the movement and of the work.

I must go back and consider the pedal: the first and third movements are so restless and conjunct in their progress that it can be used only momentarily, but the second offers every scope for it. Beethoven was always concerned that it should amplify the tone and not confuse the harmony or stifle staccato arpeggios. For the present the speed will be dictated for each movement by that at which I can play the most difficult parts —as these improve it will rise. Occasionally the metronome should be requisitioned to maintain a uniform rate, so that I do not have sections moving quicker because they are easier, and equally as it is speeded up that I keep it in check, not accelerating through excitement and getting out of control, like a rider who drops the reins and is at the mercy of his mount. The real speed, compared with Bach, is settled by tradition, and that is that the two outer movements are to be played as quickly as may be consistent with clarity and correctness. One edition suggests $\downarrow$. $= 76$ for the first and $\downarrow = 96$ for the third; these are high speeds, and if they mean that certain parts, such as the semiquavers in the third, have to be slowed down, they are too high. Besides, I feel that in the first it would be effective to have something in reserve for slightly hurrying forward at 82 to 86 and at 259 to 263; there should be no rallentando to close the exposition and only a momentary delay of the last chord at the very end. In the finale I should like a little more precision at the half closes at 20 and 21 and 78 and 79, and a real rallentando at 55 to 59, but it should not be possible to quicken anywhere unless it be the last Tempo I, and that more by contrast with the slow time immediately before it. And no rallentando or pedal at the close.

For the Adagio, ♪ = 66 is appropriate enough, yet even so the rhapsodical phrases will require to be very fast. A slight hastening would suit 31 to 34 and its repetition, and a bar or two of the return of the opening a shade slower than it originally was; and I must reflect that the marks of emphasis are not the same as elsewhere but only relative: so also with a crescendo and a forte. I wish to get the full beauty of the coda, with its throbbing syncopation, its melodic fragments below, its final farewell on the mediant at 107 and 108, and its lingering on the chord with both pedals down. Much more than all the others do these four pages afford sufficient opportunity to look into the personal refinements of interpretation, too delicate to be put down in notation. Beethoven generally reveals himself at his greatest moments in his slow movements, and some of the most searching problems he sets us are to be found in them. This one will call for much experiment—for weeks I shall have to give thought to the various qualities of touch, the tonal values, the phrasing and expression necessary to give it coherence and unity. It is not easy with the fleeting tones of the piano to sing out with rich legato and shade off at the ends such long-drawn sentences. They have to be plastically modelled, each note in its relationship to the others, and when I recall hearing at orchestral concerts how the same movements sounded, such as in the Fifth and Seventh Symphonies and the 'Emperor' Concerto, this seems impossible. I have to do my best with the movement that shows the one deficiency of the instrument.

Such are the deciding factors for the whole work: they mean that the nearer the speeds are to the suggested ones the better.

At any rate everything must be thrown off with rhythmic vitality and it is better to exaggerate the contrasts of tone than have them on a more uniform level. A lifeless performance of this music is of all sins the unforgivable one. Czerny, who knew it intimately, said that Beethoven's playing had 'tremendous power, character, unheard-of brilliance and facility.' We can quite clearly hear him in this sonata and we must follow his example.

THE ROMANTIC PIECE

For most candidates the third piece carries the interest attached to something which brings them nearer their own day: it is often programme music with a concrete title as an aid to its appreciation, and it is written in a freer and more epigrammatic style. The choice is wide and the range fascinating. It extends from the safe strains of the so-called romantic composers to the impressionism of the present and has something to suit every capacity and taste.

There are several considerations to guide the candidate in deciding his choice. The work is generally short and in ternary form, and in this connection there is a point worth mentioning: if the third part is an exact reproduction of the first part then in the examiners' estimation it makes it only two-thirds of a piece; so he would be wiser to select something that entails more preparation and more variety. Unless he is going to play it extremely well, a familiar Chopin, Schumann, or Mendelssohn work will lay him open to comparison with the traditional perfection of every great player. It will put him at a certain disadvantage right away. Besides, the examiners have just had to listen to things by Bach and Beethoven which they have known all their lives, and which however well played cannot have brought them any pleasurable sense of novelty. Now they are to be subjected to something else no less familiar and it is apt to complete the strain on their patience. Further, it must be remembered they are doomed to a similar experience for hours every day of the week, and it is exhausting work. How they welcome some new and bright piece to bring a waft of refreshment into their appointed lot! In the list there are many suitable for the purpose which are seldom or never chosen: the fact that they are on the list means they are not beyond the standard of difficulty expected. Ireland, for instance, Bax, and Moeran among our own men and noted for their integrity; Debussy, atmospheric in manner; Fauré, charmingly lyrical; Poulenc, quaintly humorous; Grovlez, attractively pianistic; Livens, lively and amusing; Albeniz, characteristically national; Medtner, romantic in idea; Rachmaninov, gently meditative. Anything by them is well written for the modern instrument and offers scope for gifts of imaginative interpretation; the candidate might find among them an opportunity to display his.

Here melody is not so obvious—it may move on two levels or it may be fragmentary; a bass such as is so assured in the two other works may not exist. From his acquaintance with harmony he may have to regard some of the progressions as unexplainable. Some of them are elliptical by omitting what is taken for granted. Discords are more prevalent and sound unpleasant when played slowly; one in the treble stave looks as though it has some form of resolution in another discord in the bass; or it may not resolve at all. They may be chords of the seventh or the ninth or variations of them with other notes added to give a blurred effect; they may be accented auxiliary notes, notes against themselves chromatically altered; or they may arise from independent figures or strands of chords moving in similar or in contrary direction. To grasp these things it is evident that a wider view of the bar has to be taken, for several bars may be required to show what is happening in any one of them. The scale may be altered to the whole-tone or to a variety of mode. Modulations are more epigrammatically done by short cut or by suggestion, or by the form of the scale. The leading note may be flattened, or its place taken by the sharpened subdominant or by chords of the seventh or the ninth. The hands may seem to move together in different keys. The time signature may vary from bar to bar; the tempo is freer and more rubato, and often a middle section is expected to quicken though not so indicated. The pedal is not marked while yet an essential feature as it gathers the fragments into a series of scintillating harmonies. Many of the old traditions seem to have been laid aside.

But the more the student plays this kind of music the more is he likely to see in it: there gradually emerges some groundwork of primary principles. Melodies and their harmonies become recognizable as they move to their destined ends, and if they collide in what is called discord they are consistent and they are being true to their purpose. For discords are relative things to be kept in their place as with a fresh set of tonal values they melt into the harmonic element. Taken at the proper speed the modernity of the piece awakens in him a special sympathy and an acknowledgment that it could not have been written in any other way.

The three pieces having been chosen, the work for the examination is settled and the responsibilities begin. Practice is the keystone of success and its effectiveness lies with the candidate himself. Where many a one falls short is in making the most profitable use of his time. He may be diligent enough in spending hours going over pages and movements, scales and arpeggios, without concentrating sufficiently on what is necessary to reach the highest standard in his power. And as the weeks pass he is apt to make it automatic, with the inevitable result that he tends to repeat the same mistakes and play everything in the same routine way without achieving distinction of style. Not by such methods does success come. Modesty in approach to his great subject is a virtue he requires to develop. He must make a habit of thinking of what he is doing and of constantly listening to himself, criticizing himself, being strict with himself. He must be unremitting in carefulness and accuracy, in preparing for every detail and every contingency, and the slow study of difficulties must continue right up to the end. The tone and the interpretation also have always to be kept under review.

His practice can be profitable only if based on a system. Two hours so spent will accomplish more than four without it. And they must be regular with nothing allowed to disturb them. If two hours are all that can be spared they may be concentrated differently for different days, the Bach and the sonata one day, scales, arpeggios, and the revision of finger exercises another day, the romantic piece and sight reading a third day, for in such an arrangement there is the gain of varied continuity compared with the loss of time in its being broken up into fragments to include everything with an eye on the clock all the while. But if the student can extend it by a third hour the sooner will he reach his goal, though he cannot forget that a further hour or two has to be set apart for the paper-work. With the necessary earnestness of purpose, he will find his mind occupied for other hours of the day with some question or other connected with the examination, and so, even away from the piano, he can go through a good deal of useful practice. At the same time he does not always appreciate that he can be too long and continuously near his work and may as the weeks pass become tired of it. By turning to other things, Bach especially, to the improvement of his playing of studies by Chopin and Moscheles, he will another day resume his chosen pieces with freshened interest. Or again he may feel that his practice of them has become stale and unprogressive. By getting outside of them and finding what others make of them he will greatly enliven it. With the scores in his hands he should make a point of hearing them played at concerts, by gramophone records or by radio, noting where his own interpretations are confirmed or may be improved. Besides, in this way their effect can be greatly enhanced by the sense of distance: this is true of everything and is not sufficiently understood. If he can hear them from a neighbouring room, from a corridor, from the open air, he will be surprised at a new and more detached conception of them: with their details refined into completeness they are enchanting, and he will take a more confident pride in them.

SOME PRINCIPLES OF TEACHING

The candidate may also have to consider the fundamental aspects of teaching his subject. He must have planned out a progressive scheme from the beginning, and he ought to have experience in adapting it to the needs of different pupils. What, he may be asked, would he do at a first lesson? He would speak simply of the mechanism of the instrument, what happens when a note is played, the effect of the right-foot pedal. He would explain the sitting position, how when the arm hangs naturally at the side it has to be lifted up and the hand half turned inwardly to lie in the right position on the keys, all under the control of the muscle at the top of the arm. The actions of the finger and the hand should be demonstrated, and the names of the notes—A, B, C, etc.—introduced. He could test the pupil's ear with high notes compared with low, a single note with two or three, loud with soft. He might then play some simple pieces, such as nursery rhymes, as examples of what a little progress will produce. He will prescribe a tutor from a list of such works familiar to him, and in it will be provided the first pieces for the future. Through its pages will be learned the elementary difficulties, finger touch, hand touch, independence of finger and hand, correctness of fingering, variations of soft and loud in each hand, easy phrasing, easy pedalling, keeping the eyes on the music. From this the pupil will progress to more advanced pieces or books of pieces, the names of which the teacher must memorize, and with the contents of which he should also be familiar; and so on through the various stages. Guidance in choosing these may be found in the syllabuses of various local examinations, for they will help him in the difficulty he often experiences of the progressive grading of pieces from one stage to another. Not until the pupil is on an elementary course should he be given simple movements from Bach's *Anna Magdalena Book* and such Romantic examples as Schumann's *Album for the Young* and Grieg's *Lyric Pieces*, Book I. It is at this point too he may be gradually introduced to scales, at first by such exercises as passing finger 1 under 2 and 3, with 1 on C and playing E above and A below with 2 and 3; the arm swinging from elbow up or down to a chord and back to the same chord, then release, hands nearer black keys, if any. Thus will major scales and broken chords with separate hands be progressively grasped, their 'tunes' becoming known and singable, and care being taken that they are always played with evenness and without stiffness. Then will the scales be done with both hands together, moving on to their relative minors and to the chromatic form.

Questions on this subject are usually put to the candidate during the practical examination.

THE EXAMINATION ROOM

The paper-work examination is an impersonal experience allowing the candidate time to collect his peace of mind and arrange his replies in the order that suits him best. The practical examination, on the other hand, is a personal interview with several distinguished strangers who expect a spontaneous response to everything they may ask. It is more of an ordeal, and no two candidates, however well prepared, approach it in the same way. One seems outwardly confident without displaying anything to justify it, another, overawed by the examiners to whom he has not been introduced, is unable to find a common ground between them and himself, another is unhappy under the strain and ready to break down. Still another comes imagining that the examiners are obsessed by certain incalculable fads of their own, and when these are not satisfied the result is failure. Too often when unsuccessful is he inclined to blame them for lack of consideration: they were brusque and asked questions not indicated in the syllabus; they talked to one another, rose and looked out of the window, sighed and noisily slumped down again, were busy writing when they should have been listening to him. By making him feel an incompetent outsider they prevented him from doing as well as he was able to do.

It is wiser and nearer the truth to regard the examiners as kindly men who too have been young and often under strain, who are themselves fine players and know the work offered thoroughly well, who as teachers and examiners are mellowed by tradition and generous in human sympathies. Having dealt with students of all stages, they do not wish them to fail and are genuinely pleased when they don't. Nor do they habitually talk or move about; but it may be they deemed it necessary to do so with a certain type of candidate so that by suggesting they were only half listening they might give him more confidence. Or perhaps they intended it to be in itself a form of test to see whether he could concentrate amid the possible distractions of a public performance. At any rate, while they recognize nervousness as a necessary ingredient in the artist, and that they have a responsibility to make allowance for it, they are so experienced as to be able to get beyond it and tell after two minutes whether the candidate has the matter in him: if he has, his habitual artistry will make itself manifest even in mistakes. Besides, for the requirements of the examination, they hold it part of its discipline to overcome the outward effects of anxiety, that one who aspires to their endorsement should be able to do so.

Nervousness is after all due to thinking of oneself rather than of the music. If real attention is given to what one is playing the self-consciousness will disappear, and for that the first essential is that the music should be thoroughly known in every detail and all its difficulties overcome. Every work so learned makes others easier and is better than a dozen half learned. It has become a habit of efficiency. The player will be alert to the responsibility of listening for and of listening to what he wishes to do: he will expect and realize. He will attend to the muscular actions as each key is put down and released at particular points of time to produce the tonal effect desired, and each subsequent key will be arranged to preserve the melodic line and the general balance. The successive sounds are the cumulative results of tonal sensation which must be remembered and constantly checked. So much is entailed as to hold the attention completely and leave no time for nervousness.

And so the candidate should approach the room believing he is prepared to meet potential well-wishers, if he will afford them the opportunity of being so. He should be fresh from resting up to the last hour, and up to the last moment he should carefully avoid listening to the experiences of previous candidates, for they will disturb his peace of mind and give him a bias in a wrong direction. He should be dressed in his best so that he may carry himself with assurance, for apart from the moral influence on him, the examiners will believe that he who is careful in such a matter will also be careful in his work. Entering with a smile and a word of greeting, he will find this secures him a valuable access of strength at the most difficult moment when it is of prime importance to get on the right terms with the situation. The first test of the examination is his personality, and though he may not feel like it he must retain his smile with its appearance of calmness. It has the effect of making him actually feel calm and do better, and may even propitiate for what may be not so good. And among the examiners who respect the pleasant appearance and manners of one proposing a professional career, it may develop into a social as well as a musical occasion.

After taking time to see that the chair is suitably adjusted and his feet are on the pedals, his duty is above all things to avoid dullness. He must play gracefully and as if he is enjoying himself, as if he loves music and especially the pieces he has brought with him. His performance of them will be vital and in the different styles appropriate to their periods, and should he, with spectacles laid aside, play from memory, he will always receive special commendation. If the accident of a wrong note occurs he must on no account come to a halt, but keep up the argument and the rhythm of the music. It is absurd to be discouraged if the examiners stop him before the end: he should rather be glad because it shows they have already come to a decision, and from the nature of his performance he will know what decision it is. If they submit to hearing the whole thing it is probably because they have not been able to make up their minds earlier. He should welcome any opportunity of discussing his pieces and their composers, the reasons why he chose them, and their particular features compared with other works in the same volume or elsewhere: it is only consistent with his musical instinct that he should have explored everything within his reach and be ready to talk enthusiastically about his special interests. That is as much as anything what is wanted.

What the examiners say or do is always to be regarded as right. It is their place, not his, to ask questions, and he ought to recognize they are not trying to show his ignorance but offering him an opportunity to display his knowledge. He must be alert to what they request and respond to it at once. Should they propose the scale of D flat he must not inquire whether they mean major or minor—if they wanted minor they would say so; D flat means major and he must not gaze at the ceiling for inspiration and play D instead. If they ask for the melodic they will not be satisfied with the harmonic. A scale in double thirds is not the same as one in thirds, nor does the dominant seventh *in* G mean the same as the dominant seventh *on* G. To their questions on technique or teaching he should not reply in monosyllables as if he has no hope of telling them anything new. What they want to find out is whether he will recognize the difficulties of his own students and be able to explain them. And so he should treat the examiners as his students for the time being and frankly and concisely elaborate a simple homily on each point raised, illustrating it on the piano, bringing forward something to show his experience, and if he can introduce a touch of humour into the situation so very much the better. Certainly there is scope for it in the test when an examiner plays part of one of the pieces with intentional mistakes, not only of notes but of phrasing, touch, lack of rhythm or expression, even of sitting wrongly on his chair. These the candidate has to point out and correct, with such advice as to encourage the hope of bringing about an improvement. He is now the examiner and quite easily can he turn it into a hilarious episode.

He has at any rate laid in a stock of everything necessary for every demand and he must put it all in the window. For at the back of what ought to be a very pleasant occasion, he has to remember that it is primarily a business engagement between him and the examiners, in which he must strive to get full value for his part in it. This, they will feel, is a young man to be encouraged : distinction already marks his work and if he continues on the same lines he will merit still further success. Meeting him has been a pleasure. He has brought a gleam of light into their long day and they are grateful for it. Only an occasional candidate leaves them in his debt, and for him it is a good augury as to the result.

The diploma when it has been achieved must not be regarded by the holder as an end in itself, beyond which he is content to make no further progress. Should he do so, then his playing will decline and he will be living in the past; ultimately the most he can say is that during a half-hour one day twenty years ago he was able to show he had reached a certain stage. He could not attempt to do it again and its value is discounted. But if he holds it as an assurance that up to that point his progress has been in the right direction and as an impetus to further pursuit of an endless subject, it will have been a success. The initial labour is past and the rest will have authority behind it. He is only beginning to enter into his inheritance as an artist. He should range through the repertoire of his instrument, go to concerts to hear as much music as he can and note the differences in its interpretation. He should keep up to date with modern criticism, and through a good musical journal learn what is being done outside his own world. If his reading recommends a piece of music of whatever kind, he should find it out—what many never trouble to do; it is the fruit of experience and it will add to his musicianship, which is as important as his technique. And what is even more important, he should find where his particular bent lies, the particular composer or style he favours, and pursue it towards its perfection. Thus by becoming a specialist will he develop his own personality, and from henceforth will his playing be a source of intellectual pleasure to himself and to all who hear him.

Diplomas in Organ Playing

THE most comprehensive diplomas in organ playing are those awarded as Associate and Fellow of the Royal College of Organists, and what may be said of them will cover the regulations for those granted by other colleges and academies. They each require a special paper and practical examination. These may vary slightly in detail from time to time, but the general conception of musicianship which they maintain remains substantially the same. And so do the fundamental principles of care and thoroughness in preparation already outlined for the pianoforte diplomas.

For the Associateship there are in addition ear tests, consisting of (1) writing from dictation five three-part chords of equal duration, selected from diatonic triads and their inversions and the chord of the dominant seventh in root position. The key will be announced, the key-chord sounded, and the passage will be played three times. For this the candidate has to concentrate all his listening, and his familiarity with sol-fa will prove helpful. The first chord must be got right: it may be different from what might be expected, such as an inversion of that on the dominant. He should try at once on the first hearing to make sure of the two outside parts with simple dots on the staves and the few figures below to indicate the inversions and dominant seventh. If he can memorize, as he ought to, five chords, with the third part consisting usually of the thirds of the chords almost automatically filling in itself, he will easily have them completed with the third hearing. The other ear test (2) is to write from dictation a melodic phrase not exceeding four bars of some form of simple time, under the same conditions as at (1). It is of the first importance to make sure of the opening note of the melody and the point of the

bar where it enters. The melody may contain modulations and awkward intervals. Another difficulty lies in notes of different lengths from dots, ties, and rests, and it may be solved by carefully noting the beats of the bar and the fractions into which the beats are divided. This may be simplified by marking the beats, according to their number, below the bars, thus: |——————————————|————————————————|
  1   2   3   4   1   2   3   4
and inserting the notes that come within each beat. In both these tests special attention should be given to the minor key.

The paper-work for the Associateship consists of two sessions, of three hours each, of harmony and counterpoint, as follows:

1. To a given treble part (with words) are to be added two vocal parts in contrapuntal style, with suggested openings for the added parts.

Assuming that the groundwork is solidly built on knowledge and practice of harmony and counterpoint, as it most certainly must be, there are two highly important considerations to be affirmed in this as in all the tests of these examinations. One is that the candidate should be able to hear mentally what he writes; the other is that the harmonic framework must always be kept simple—elaboration should not be inherent in the framework but should be imposed upon it. In this particular test the writing is to be contrapuntal, that is in melodies rather than in blocks of chords, and the vocal line of each part is to be carefully designed with due thought given to the spacing of the harmony. Effective use should be made of imitation, but only as far as the imitation is not at the expense of the harmonic structure. The treatment is not to be modal unless the given treble part suggests it, and the allotment of the words, especially when in doubt, is to be indicated. It must end in the key in which it begins, but there should be no need to add that the compasses of the voices have always to be kept in mind, and that care must be exercised here and throughout to insert the necessary accidentals; yet both matters are often overlooked.

2. A melody is to be harmonized for four voices in the style of a Bach chorale.

For this it is necessary to be familiar not only with Bach's style and technique, but particularly with his treatment of discords: diatonic and chromatic discords wherever possible add greatly to the effect. Passing-notes and suspensions should be freely but correctly employed, and they should be distributed through the voices to add to their interest. Watch has to be kept for any potential changes of key. It is always to be remembered that words are intended to be used by all the voices, and consequently a note will have to be repeated instead of being written as a long note. Here again there must be no going beyond the normal compasses of the voices.

3. A two-part invention of not less than eighteen bars is to be written in the style of Bach. The opening bar or two will be given, and phrasing and expression are to be added.

In an invention a figure is worked out imitatively in contrapuntal style after the manner of Bach's fifteen inventions in two parts, which are the best examples to follow. It is to be in binary form, the first part ending in a related key, the second part beginning in that key with the opening imitations inverted and ending in the tonic key. Any momentary modulation in the first part, such as to the relative minor on the way to the dominant, will be reproduced in the second part by the supertonic minor in returning to the tonic: the relationship of the two pairs of keys being thus kept the same. In the minor key the first part may end in the relative major or the dominant major. Special attention has to be given to the harmonic basis, sometimes only implied in two parts, to the rhythm of the chordal changes, and to the tonality. All dissonances should be resolved. Practice in this kind of writing should extend beyond eighteen bars and even to three parts, again according to Bach's example, and must be frequent enough to acquire speed and facility.

4. A brief instrumental piece in eighteenth-century dance

form is to be composed for three string instruments or piano, the opening three or four bars being given.

Here it is, of course, necessary to know the distinctive characteristics of these old dances, such as the saraband and the minuet, the style, the rhythm of each, the beat of the bar on which it begins. These may be exemplified in Bach's English and French Suites and his partitas. They are all in binary form with the two sections repeated. The writing must have form and balance of phrases, and the process of modulation must be natural and carefully arranged. If the strings are used the compass of each has to be watched, the special point being its lowest note, and the bowing is naturally to be inserted.

5. A period of the history of English church music is prescribed, and of three questions set one is to be answered.

The question must be carefully read and understood. What is wanted for answer is not merely biographical detail or memorized portions from books, but a knowledge of representative music of the period, with personal opinions on it and quotations from it. Everything must be relevant and to the point and expressed in good literary style, by which the candidate will be judged as much as by his knowledge of history. It must be repeated that here as throughout the examination the handwriting and the musical notation should be clear and correct in every detail. Time should be reserved for revision and for any necessary amendments.

This equally applies to the question on general musical history set in the Fellowship examination.

For the Fellowship two papers of three hours each are based on the following lines:

1. To a given subject a fugal exposition is to be written in four parts for strings or organ, as specified.

Here it is essential to get the correct answer to the subject and the key underlying it. Continuous movement must be contrived between the end of the subject and the entry of the answer. Unless for sufficient reason, codettas are best avoided. The counter-subject must have individuality and be invertible only at the octave or fifteenth, but it should not cross over the answer. The freer parts require to be given contrasting characters and the rhythms to be made progressive: that is, they should be written in fugal counterpoint. The whole thing, being in four parts, will extend to sixteen or eighteen bars. As before, if strings are employed, the compass of each must be remembered and the bowing added throughout.

2. Gives a choice of writing (*a*) a short choral prelude for organ on a given tune; or (*b*) three variations and coda on a given ground bass for organ.

Both these forms require invention and ingenuity, musical feeling, and a sense of style. The harmonic framework has to be logically directed and the part-writing has to have a natural flow. In the choral prelude each line of the tune is preceded by three-part imitational entries arising out of its opening notes, after this manner:

The lines of the tune are consequently separated by two or three bars of rest, and are accompanied contrapuntally. The last line of the tune brings the prelude to an end. In the ground bass the interest must be contrasted and cumulative, but it should not be allowed to become too elaborate. The limit of three variations compels the candidate to the more striking artistic devices, such as rhythmical figures, passing-notes, suspensions and appoggiaturas, imitations. The harmony should change with each variation: the coda may invert the bass or be built on a pedal point with a contrapuntal climax above.   Either scheme should be a finished piece of writing which it would be a pleasure to hear in performance.

3. About ten bars are to be written for string quartet, the complete first violin part being given, while a suggested opening of two bars may be used or not at the option of the candidate.

Here it is more essential than ever that the candidate should be able to hear optically what he writes, and that his harmonic background should be kept simple so that by avoiding the ever-present danger of becoming too complex there may be fuller opportunity for melodious treatment of the parts.   He ought to conform to the suggestions underlying the given bars and continue in a good instrumental style.   The range and distribution of the parts must be carefully considered with a due appreciation of the value of rests.   Their phrasing must be expressive.   Modulations have to be suitable and convincingly realized.   Imitations and other devices are good if they do not disturb the style, which is harmonic counterpoint with a touch of lightness.   It is a style totally distinctive from that for voices, while the agility and the wider range of strings allow of much greater freedom of movement.

4. Gives another choice of writing (*a*) a brief motet or madrigal in three parts in the style of Palestrina or of the Tudor school, as specified, one part with words being given, and two opening bars suggested; or (*b*) a short part-song or unaccompanied anthem in four parts, an outer part being given with words; or, if preferred, an original part-song or anthem to the given words.

For the motet, the student must familiarize himself with the technique, the rhythms, and the idioms of sixteenth-century counterpoint and especially with the styles of Palestrina and the Tudor school, of which there are plenty of examples for the purpose.   The rhythms are free.   Points of imitation are expected to be realized, and method must guide the entries and endings of the parts.   The words will entail the repetitions of notes.

The part-song is a piece of modern composition following a fixed design with a solid harmonic basis and a tonality founded on a well-thought-out plan of keys. It must not be a series of commonplace chords, but have independent part-writing with melodic interest in each part. Imagination is to be shown in the treatment of the words and coherence in its purpose. Long practice is necessary to achieve facility in this searching test.

5. A short passage from an orchestral score is to be arranged for the organ on three staves.

The purpose of this test is primarily to write an organ piece, and it is essential that the candidate should be able to recognize how the score will sound on the orchestra and how its effect will be realized in his arrangement for the instrument. For this a knowledge of orchestral technique, particularly of the sounds of the transposing instruments and of the idioms in reproducing certain types of writing, is necessary. The speed and special features of the piece are to be considered; the melodic lines and important entries that have to be brought out are to be given their places. The arrangement must be kept simple with everything superfluous omitted. Resource has to be shown in the spacing of the chords and in allowing for the mechanical actions forced on the player as they arise from variations of tone. It is to be written naturally and expressively for the organ. There has long been division of opinion as to the playing of orchestral music on it, and this test gives a sanction to doing so.

Should the candidate find the time insufficient for him to complete the paper, say in the last question, he must indicate the first few bars complete, the outside parts and any inner melodies, and changes of manuals; everything, in other words, but what may be automatically filled in. His purpose must be shown in all the vital things.

THE PRACTICAL EXAMINATION

Many of the principles for the practical examination already advocated to candidates for the pianoforte diplomas apply equally to those for the organ diplomas. The keyboards of both instruments are the same and so are many of their technical problems. This is true to such a degree that the organ student should strengthen his technique at the piano to get facility in finger work, and thus gain an easy mastery of the manual difficulties. He should so develop his playing that as far as possible he has no need to look at his hands. This will further save him much time he would otherwise have to spend at the organ.

But there are special features in organ playing that call for concentrated attention at the instrument itself. By its very nature it requires clean honest fingering: with no sustaining pedal and the tone being independent of the touch, it has no means of covering up a deficiency; it offers no compromise and is in the open all the time. An accidental movement of an adjacent note may produce no effect on the piano, but it will on the organ, and security can be acquired only by making sure to depress the note right in the middle. And as note follows note there must be a compromise of rhythm. Bach has many scalar passages grouped according to hands, instead of beats, such as in the Toccata in C:

and it is necessary to mark the beats, for though they are rhapsodical flights they must be rhythmical. On this most unrhythmical of instruments, it should always be possible to say how many beats are in the bar. And this should be so no matter how high the speed.

Take a scale like that in Bach's Prelude in D:

Brushing aside everything that has gone before, it flashes up as with the swish of a sword to the salute of the chord of D with its third at the point. On the piano half-pedalling might help to suggest more bustle and cover a defect, but not here. With the foot already placed for the pedal bass to the chord, the scale requires complete attention and the most exact playing. Still more does the last page of the accompanying fugue, where with every defence down it boldly lunges forward and the slightest slip would spell disaster. This is virtuoso playing as exacting as any the piano has to offer.

Again, as arpeggios are broken chords, it is most important to regard them in their original forms: it not only simplifies the playing of them but also reveals their plain harmonic procedure. The elaborate fantasia, 'Come, Holy Ghost, Lord God,' is an instance of this; so is the long choral prelude, 'Glory be to God on High,' where such a passage as this:

should be regarded in the right hand as:

and the left as:

thus reducing the playing of the passage to the changing positions of the hands. In echo effects, such as those in the Toccata in D minor:

the simple arpeggios are to be practised softly as chords, all on one manual—they give the lie of each hand; then again as chords in going from one manual to the other, which must be done accurately without touching other notes. The act of going and returning quickly is the difficulty. The same applies to the responsive phrases in the middle of the Toccata in F.

The manual parts should be further practised at the organ with special care for leaps to notes and chords, which are more difficult than on the piano, and for a part that passes from one hand to the other, marking it if necessary and watching the awkwardness it often produces. The pedal part has to be taken alone, for it must be equally sure, and every footing that is to be remembered should be indicated. The complete independence of hands and feet can be achieved by a study of Bach's Six Sonatas, as well as a further insight into the composer's most gracious style. It will generally be found that the treacherous points in a fugue are those where the pedal enters, for the time must be maintained as if they were as easy as the rest. In Bach's 'Great' G minor Fugue, such a passage as:

and there are a number of others, requires constant attention and going over with hands alone, with each hand and
pedal, and the three together, slowly right up to the end.

For both diplomas the tests at the organ are: (1) set pieces,
(2) sight reading, (3) vocal score reading, and (4) transposition, while for the Fellowship is added the harmonization
of a hymn tune or chorale and extemporization on the tune.
For the Associateship two pieces are set, one of the Bach period,
the other modern; for the Fellowship three pieces are set, two
of them generally modern.

1. The candidate will carefully select the pieces most suitable to him, and in them and in the tests he ought to prepare
himself beyond what will be required.   He has always to be
critical of his own performance, concentrating on special
points, such as ornaments, and trying to get them up to a
quicker speed than need be.   Alterations of manuals and of
stops are due only after the actual playing has been thought
out in every detail and is confident in all the parts.   A matter
often forgotten is arranging to turn over the pages by the left
hand with the least interruption to the flow of the music.
Towards the end, when the pieces should be more or less
memorized, he should act at the organ as if the examiners were
present.   He ought, in addition, to study the form of each piece,
analyse the fugue in its various entries and episodes, observe
wherein a sonata movement departs from the classical

tradition. The style too and historical position of the composer are matters for his consideration. In these as in all his preparations he should preserve a sense of inquiry and try to be worthy of all that his noble but much abused instrument is able to give him.

The candidate for this examination differs from every candidate in another subject because of the fact that no two organs are alike, and the stops and mechanical appliances may be in differect positions from those to which he is accustomed. This places him at a certain disadvantage. He must procure a specification of the college organ and make himself completely familiar with its features. With this before him he has to consider what stops he proposes to use at various points, where they are and what movements will be necessary for either hand in getting to them, what the thumb and toe pistons do, whether they are interchangeable, whether those for the Great affect the pedals too, where the Swell to Great is, the Great to Pedal, and if the pedal-board extends to high G how this will disturb his playing when he is not accustomed to it. If he has an opportunity of previous practice, he should waste no time in exploring what he will not require but devote every moment to such essential things as these. If he has no such opportunity, as is the case with many a candidate from a distance, he must on no account at the examination sound some of the stops to find their quality, but understand that they are of the standard kind. He will have to depend on his knowledge of the specification and plan for safety.

At the examination it has to be recognized that everything is expected to pass off as if at a public performance. It must not stop and go back because of a slip, but be steady and continuous. Technical efficiency, rhythmic grip, and absolute control of the instrument are of paramount importance. The speed will be that at which the candidate can feel secure at the more dangerous parts; the rhythm must be maintained by a free use of staccato. In music of the Bach period the phrasing is to be consistently followed in both manuals and pedals; if a crescendo by the Swell pedal would disturb the phrasing of the pedal part, it should be omitted.

The registration should be limited and simple, and if a change of stops would cause a slowing down it ought to be left out. Variety can be obtained by a move to another manual, though there is no occasion, for instance, to solo an upper entry of a fugue subject. In a Trio, where the oboe in one of the parts is to be avoided, variety can lie in a simple exchange of manuals at the end of a section. It is too often forgotten that the organ, compared with the piano, has a rigid tone which can soon become tiring, and if it be necessary to increase it care must be exercised, for it means a sudden rise in the block of sound with a corresponding assault on the ear of the hearer. A useful rule for minimizing the change, while playing on the Great coupled with the Swell, is: when adding a Great stop open the Swell pedal, when adding a Swell stop close the Swell pedal. In neither case should the new tone encroach upon a note or chord, but it should take place between phrases. The adding of two stops doubles the responsibility, and consequently there is no need to indulge in heavy reeds or the full organ, for these can be proportionately trying in a comparatively small room. It is sufficient to suggest them, and their reality can be taken for granted. The general tone is to be appropriate, clear and bright rather than loud, for after all the quality of the playing is more important than the pulling out of more stops. This older type of music will never be dull or mechanical if unfolded with a broad legato tempered by phrasing, which is the true style of the organ.

A warning must be given against two real dangers that may waylay the anxious candidate towards the end of a lively piece, both of which can be well exemplified by Bach's 'Gigue' Fugue in G. One is that he may allow himself to be carried off by excitement, especially here at the jauntiness of the rhythm of two notes grouped in threes, and so lose command of the time. The other danger is that he may be tempted to fill in the chording with duplicated notes to make it sound bigger and grander.   This is another form of excitement.   Bach's fugue draws to a climax with gathering exhilaration in all the parts, and closes in this manner:

It seems a disappointingly thin conclusion to what has gone before, and many venture to improve it with something more worthy, thus:

There are two arguments against this: one that Bach did not write it, the other that the chords, as he knew full well, are really expanded several octaves by the various stops of different pitch.   This is what he wanted and we must give it to him.

Both these tendencies are to be resisted, which means that the candidate has to gain control not only of his instrument but of himself.

In the modern piece he will have to make sure of not mis-reading the text.   He must judge the tempo and any definite change in it that may occur in a later section.   At no point should the time be too strictly kept, but it should be guided by imagination and a subtle flexibility.   In this expansive music the candidate must conceive the expression appropriate to its romantic nature.   He will round off the phrases sensitively according to an intelligent view of their shape and design. Its atmosphere will be enhanced by a tender regard for its dis-cords and chromatic modulations, by constant listening and a tasteful scheme of registration.   Good taste will avoid all exotic combinations of stops and, of course, the Tremulant, which can have only an adverse effect on the examiners.   The tone must fit the style.   If the composer asks for particular stops it is better to adopt them, but if he bases them on continental resources not available here, they should be modi-fied so that an equally musical effect may result.   Care must be taken for the balance of tone, which may often be put right by the simple expedient of the Swell pedal, as with a solo and its accompaniment.   A point frequently overlooked is that crescendos and diminuendos are intended by the composer to be taken gradually.

2. The tests are the parts of the practical examination which are always inadequately done, owing to insufficient preparation arising either from a distaste for them or from an equally foolish idea that they are only of secondary importance. For such candidates there is no possible hope of success.

With each test it is permissible to take a brief glance over it before beginning, but too much advantage must not be taken of this. It is specially necessary with sight reading since the stop indications, the changes of manuals depending on whether the Swell or Choir swell pedals should be open or closed, the entry or silence of the pedal part, and the variations in the expression have all to be scrupulously followed. The piece has a metronome rate also which is to be accepted as a guide to the time: for this it would suffice to be familiar with a certain rate, such as ♩ = 60, and quickly calculate from it accordingly—90, for instance, would be a half quicker than 60. It is better, however, to play rather slower and correctly than up to speed with mistakes. The key and the time signatures must be firmly fixed in the mind, so as to be ready without looking back for any changes they may undergo. The sense of key will recognize accidentals as lasting for the bar and not beyond it. In this test concentration on the page, looking ahead, and rapid thinking in phrases and not from note to note are very necessary. The time is to be strict, notes and rests are to be given their correct values, and the performance is to be smooth and continuous; in addition it must have style suitable to the spirit of the music and be fluent in interpretation, rhythm, and stop management. Practice for it should be concentrated on works of similar difficulty to the set pieces.

3. Vocal score reading is a test in four lines with three G clefs and bass clef for the Associateship, and treble, alto, tenor, and bass clefs for the Fellowship. For the first, two clefs are in use; for the second, four, including two C clefs. Only practice of both forms from published books of exercises will afford a real grip of a test which is often badly done, and as in neither case are the pedals to be used the practice can be done mostly on the piano. Begin with two parts, then three, and lastly four, thinking of the parts as melodies, which means contrapuntally rather than harmonically. The movement of the inner parts, especially where they cross over each other or the two outer parts, requires particular attention. Again the key must be kept steadfastly in the mind so as to avoid the need to look back to the signature: the eyes are to be at the

G

place on the page the whole time. The test is expected to be confidently played, not too slowly or too quickly, but at the prescribed time and without stopping at a mistake.

4. For transposition, in which the pedals are to be used, a familiarity with every key is necessary, and practice should specialize in going from a key in sharps to one in flats, and vice versa. If it begins with simple, well-known hymn tunes a mistake may easily be recognized, for the tune has to sound the same in whatever key it may be played. Tunes in minor keys require special attention, as also do modulations and diatonic discords. The bass part must be secure and it is better to regard the harmonies up from the bass than down from the melody. The hymn tune set for the examination may begin with some other chord than the tonic and the progressions are often different from what might be expected. For the Fellowship a simple passage of organ music on three staves is set, and for this practice has to be extended to pieces of a similar kind until fluency is acquired. This test especially must be done at once with confident ease and, like the others, at the time indicated. The occasion for transposition in the work of an organist will be an actual performance, in which the piece is to sound exactly the same as in the original key.

5. The additional test for Fellowship, in which a given hymn tune or chorale is to be harmonized and followed by a short extemporization on it, is important as affording an opportunity for spontaneous musicianship. Facility must first be achieved in harmonizing the hymn tune. This has to display readiness in seizing its character, recognizing the key, the possibility of modulations, and the approach to them by appropriate chords. The ideal to be worked for is the treatment of the Bach chorale in Question 2 of the paper for Associates. Again the time is to be as indicated. The pedals are to be used.

In the extemporization, the severest trial of the practical examination, basic keyboard harmony in simple chords is to be used. It must not be an aimless wandering about with only a slight connection with the theme provided: on the other hand it must not overdo the theme. It has to reveal imagination. The candidate ought to have several formal plans and means of treatment, including modulations, ready to hand, for he will always find it possible to use one of them. It may be a binary or better still a ternary form, with the middle section in a related key, and he should write out short pieces on previous subjects to see what he can do with them and how far he can carry their development. This will help him too in acquiring the necessary spontaneity at the examination. In an extemporization in simple triple time he would be expected to reach to about thirty bars, in compound triple time to about half that number.

Suppose the given theme to be this:

On the first impulse he might begin thus:

But the theme is generally chosen to offer a chance for imitation, even of canon, in which two parts will suffice. He should not start too quickly but consider for a moment such possibilities as these. The above theme does suggest imitational entries, which might set off thus:

This is much better. The subject will indeed lend itself to
further appearances and imitations, and it can be easily
inverted at such a point as may be leading back to the return
of the original key:

or at the actual return of the key. This is a device which is
always received with approval. There should be plenty of
rests to avoid too much of four parts. With the outside parts
kept solidly correct, either expressed or understood, the
extemporization should be relevant and result in a piece of
logical development, complete in its build-up and climax.
The player must listen to his own competent progress and
enjoy himself, letting the parts flow as he wills them to arrive
at destinations which he can always accept for his purpose. He
will instinctively avail himself of the resources at his command,

for in carefully changing the tone by stop or manual he can be effectively enterprising. Codas ought to be brief and bear reference to something in the theme: pedal points are to be avoided. It is important, as throughout the examination, that the pedal part should not have only a soft 16-foot tone, but be made distinctive by the addition of an 8 foot or by being coupled to the manual.

The Fellowship is the most searching of all diploma examinations in this country. It demands natural gifts, long preparation in every department, and the ability to do easily and completely whatever may be asked from the whole complicated range of the organist's activities. It certifies the holder to be a capable and resourceful player and to be an all-round artist who is also a pianist and a composer in various styles with a knowledge of choral, chamber, and orchestral music, about which he can express himself intelligently for the profit of others: one, that is, who by continuing to develop his accomplishments is able to take a leading part in the musical life of the sphere to which he may be called.

Diplomas in Singing

CANDIDATES for these diplomas have the option of entering as teachers or as performers.

For the teacher's examination three numbers are to be prepared, and they must include a recitative. These are not to be sung mechanically; nor need they be, for the candidate has their choice in his own hands from a wide selection, and they should be such as can be interpreted with all his force of mind and body as well as of voice. In them he has to show the practical results of the precepts he enforces on his students.

The rest of the examination is concerned with teaching. An unfamiliar song and recitative are to be analysed and used for a demonstration lesson; with them opportunity will be given to enlarge on the physical conditions underlying singing and the mechanism of sound production. Questions may also be asked on the teaching of technique and interpretation, the principles of studying a song and its style, the choice of music for various stages of development, and on the solos of standard oratorios and operas. The candidate may further be expected to play and transpose a simple accompaniment.

The questions on the physical conditions of singing will concern the operative or motive power of the voice in the diaphragm muscle, the ribs, lungs, trachea, bronchi, the intercostal muscles and their connections and purposes; the organs used in singing, the larynx and the muscles and cartileges associated with it, their influence in breathing, the pharynx, hard and soft palates, tongue, teeth, lips, mouth and nose, their use and misuse in forming the breath into tone; the different compasses of the registers employed; production of the voice, resonance, diction, pronunciation, enunciation, intonation, expression, and phrasing, the causes of and cures for bad breathing, forcing up of the registers, bad tone, tremolo, slurring. In his study of these subjects the candidate should prepare his oral explanations by writing little essays or synopses of each of them.

His answers are to be concise and such as will reveal a sound training and a practical knowledge rather than a study of physiological books. They should be enforced by relevant illustrations. But what is of still greater importance is that to this knowledge must be added experience in teaching, for it is on such experience that most of the questions are based. They are asked with a view to eliciting personal opinions and mature principles in dealing with various voices and different types of nature in students, of whom no two are alike. And as a pleasant manner and enthusiasm are necessary for a successful teacher, so must they be shown throughout the examination.

In the assessing of performers, the standard and scope of singing is of a higher order and is to be such as would be expected on a classical concert platform. The general requirements are four or five works, including a recitative, chosen from given lists according to the particular voice, and of these two are to be sung from memory. Foreign songs may be done in the languages of their titles, but at least one should be in English. The candidate is expected also to read at sight, for this is sometimes a regrettable weakness even in a good singer. He is further responsible for his own accompanist.

The works, for the choice of which special marks are allotted according to their varied and representative characters, will depend on his individual gifts and must reveal to advantage various aspects of his technical and interpretative skill. His tastes may lie in reflective songs, or *lieder*, or dramatic arias, but in whatever direction there is plenty of scope for their exercise. In all these things he ought to be pianist enough to play his own accompaniments in private practice, for they are inseparable from the voice parts.   Surely too there should be no great difficulty in his memorizing two songs, and if he can do so with the whole five so much the fairer are his prospects. What he is chiefly judged by is the quality and volume of voice, breath control, intonation, blending of registers, diction and pronunciation, the clarity of words—equally in a foreign tongue—interpretation and emotional insight, phrasing and expression, time and rhythm, and the general impression he creates, which can be built up by a well-conceived plan with the favourite and more personally effective numbers reserved to the end.   Years of study as an artist, experienced guidance, and daily practice are essential for the candidate to make the impression a favourable one.

There are two features which are peculiar to this examination.   One is that the music for it, compared with that for other subjects, is in touch with the human scene: it is all programme music.   It deals with love, life, and destiny, having a special appeal to the singer's sympathies, and affording opportunities for the full development of his expressive powers.   Indeed there is material enough in it for the exercise of his gifts of mind and soul.   The items are all different, and each is to be unfolded in the style befitting its character.   They give him a story to tell, a thought to illuminate, a scene to portray—he may even have the advantage of a piece of humour to relate, with all of which he takes his hearers into his confidence, and in so far as each number means something to him, such will he make it for them.   Besides, they usually display the best powers of the composer, for however revolutionary he may be in his instrumental writing, in this he must be rational because of the limits imposed upon him by the voice and by the words.   It includes some of the most beautiful music in existence, and the singer can never grow tired of it.   Thrice happy should he be whose daily portion is the canticles of Bach and Handel, the arias of Mozart, the songs of Schubert and Brahms, the fresh flights of the moderns, for he dwells in an enchanted world.

The other feature, for which also additional marks are reserved, is the consideration of deportment, because of the publicity and direct appeal of the concert platform. It is all carefully watched—the candidate's tasteful dress, his walking on to the platform, standing with head erect while the opening prelude is being played, his pleasant expression during the song, his remaining on the platform when it is finished, his courtesy towards the accompanist, his continuing to face his audience, his waiting for the next item without wondering what to do with himself, and so through the rest of the programme, his bow at the end though there has been never a murmur of applause. That is part of the test and he must throughout suggest complete reliance on himself. And such he ought to have. He has come armed with a number of treasures of his own choice, in each of which he has to assume a new personality, and if he has thoroughly prepared them in every detail, his self-reliance will be more than a suggestion: it will be a reality. And that will have the effect of making his audience feel a pleasurable reliance on him.

Diplomas in School Music

THE examination for these diplomas is a practical one for teachers, and it shows the important place that has been granted to the increasing potentialities of school music.

It generally consists of three parts: (1) aural training and appreciation, (2) voice culture and class singing, and (3) a paper on the principles of teaching. As in all diplomas experience is an important consideration, so here the candidate must have spent some years in dealing with school conditions.

For (1) a class is provided and a complete lesson is to be given to them on a subject associated with aural training, such as pitch, scales and keys, time and rhythm, intervals, modulation, melody-making. The candidate will be required to play and comment on an imaginative piece of his own choice which will be of musical interest to the class, to conduct a melody with regard to its phrasing and expression, and to answer questions on the teaching of ear training and musical appreciation. Then there is keyboard work in playing a slow movement of Beethoven, sight reading, harmonizing a melody, modulation and extemporization of phrases leading to cadences and of short pieces after the manner of classical dances; also playing the melody and accompaniment of a unison song. After sight-singing follow aural tests in writing a melody, a rhythm, two parts, four-part chords, phrasing and expression of a melody played by the examiner; and finally to identify extracts from well-known standard works. The aural tests and those at the piano have already been touched upon here under other diplomas. Most marks are given for the class lesson (coupled with the questions on teaching), and for the harmonization, modulation, and extemporization.

To a candidate who is accomplished in aural tests, the first problem is to get to the elementary principles in guiding children from the beginning. He has to understand difficulties for them which do not exist for himself, and the brief steps which lead progressively from one point to another. An extensive literature is, however, at his hand to help him. At the examination the question of discipline is sufficiently tested by the interest and enthusiasm of the candidate in unfolding the lesson to the class.

For (2) a class of adults is provided and is to be given a lesson on a two-part song provided forty minutes earlier, as well as exercises to improve their singing. The candidate has to bring songs in one, two, and three parts, sing from memory the first verse of one of the unison songs, pointing the melody on the sol-fa modulator, and discuss aspects of the teaching of class singing and repertoire. He will further play the prepared accompaniments of two songs, one of which will be performed by the class; read at sight an accompaniment, a three-part vocal score written on three staves with treble clefs, and transpose; also sing melodies at sight and the lower of two parts while the upper is played by the examiner. Among these activities most marks are allotted to the class-singing lesson (coupled with conducting), and for the prepared accompaniments (including the direction of the class from the piano).

Before conducting the lesson on the two-part song it is necessary for the candidate to see that the choir are grouped together according to the two parts. He should be prepared with the fundamental points he will expect from them whatever they sing—such as posture, attention to his direction, breathing, voice production, intonation, and enunciation—and make up his mind during the forty minutes as to the special ones called for in the actual song they are to sing. It is known to the choir: it is new to him; yet he must have grasped it thoroughly enough to detect errors the choir may even intentionally introduce, and have everything to say that will have bearing on their attack, blend, inter-relationship between the two parts and their interpretation. The standard he should set before himself is that prevailing at a musical festival, and there ought to be as a result a notable improvement in the choir's performance during the short time he is with them. The same should be true of the accompanied song, in which he has to play clearly and rhythmically so as to guide them in entries and give them adequate support while singing. With a look or a gesture he can indicate to them the necessary changes of time or of expression.

Throughout the examination, but particularly in his dealings with the choir, he must avoid being dull or serious, but be bright, sympathetic, and imaginative, and if possible he should lighten the proceedings with humour. He has to give the appearance of being perfectly free and confident though among complete strangers, for his personality is very much under survey.

The paper on the principles of teaching (3) comprises questions on elementary psychology and method as they apply to class singing, aural training, and musical appreciation. Here a study of books can afford only partial help, and the candidate has more of an opportunity of showing his experience and expressing the opinions he may have formed from it. The subjects he should specially consider are the mechanism of the act of singing, the various organs used, the hard and soft palates, the head voice and its compass, economy of breathing, lateral breathing and the curing of faults; vocal exercises for classes of different ages, vowel sounds producing pure quality of tone, exercises for flexibility and resonance, for sight reading, the singing of consonants, developing a sense of time. Questions may also be asked for personal views on the repertoire of songs, including those of the Elizabethan composers and folk-songs, on the division of voices according to parts and the making of them blend, on the usefulness of broadcast lessons and of orchestral concerts for schools, and on the differences among classes, including the children who are tonally deaf and those who are inattentive and do not like the singing lesson.

The teacher of school music has it in his power to be a great force for good, though its effect may be slow in realizing itself. He has for the most part to deal with raw material, which has not chosen to come and listen to him, but is there simply by the regulations of the curriculum. Children are not able to express themselves on the subject beyond their evident pleasure in the short and disconnected times he is with them. And so he has to work in faith, hoping that he is at least creating for them at their impressionable age a taste and a respect for what is fine in music, which may linger with them for the rest of their days. But he cannot assess the good he is doing: the individual is lost in the class. Then one day he finds his hope realized when a small residue remains with him for further study, or one of the others, now reached maturity, recalls the past and expresses a word of grateful appreciation. Perhaps there are others of them who feel the same. It is a happy thought, sufficient to encourage him and assure him that it has been much worth while.

Diplomas in Theory

THE examination for a diploma in theory corresponds with that of teacher in other subjects. It is conducted by paper and by viva voce, the rudiments of music being taken for granted. For the paper work is required a knowledge of harmony in four or five parts, counterpoint for voices or instruments, free counterpoint, double counterpoint two in one with the addition of a free part, canon and fugue in four parts. A piano accompaniment may also be expected.

This is a lot of work and it is intended for those who are specially versed in the theoretical side of music. It should scarcely be necessary to say that they who have travelled so far should be able to hear what they write; if they had not the ability to begin with, they must surely have acquired it by now. It is quite essential. For even for them the great difficulty lies in having to do everything in the time allotted. Most of them could accomplish it comfortably if they had double the time: but that is not sufficient. Speed is as important as knowledge. It is a test in facility which comes only with long practice in each type of question that is set, and it should not matter what the form of a question may be—the manner of answering it has to be ready to hand. It must be attacked at once without taking time to achieve individual effects or originality. It has to become almost mechanical.

In vocal writing in five parts, the treble or the tenor is better to double than any of the other parts; in string writing the viola is the best to double. The two outside parts should be kept well separated to afford freer movement to the others, and the parts may cross for more melodic movement and to avoid monotony. While the fifth part adds considerable complication, the rules of four-part writing are not relaxed; consecutives, for instance, even by contrary motion, are still not allowed. Again it is to be remembered that the styles of expression for voices and for instruments are entirely different. The addition of a free part to a double counterpoint has little freedom, since it must fit in with the strictness of the two given parts: it can be a task of considerable difficulty, but it may be eased by the harmonies changing more quickly and the treatment of auxiliary and dissonant notes falling by step being less stringent. A fugue calls for experience that will be instantly available in practice. The exposition must be given and at least an outline of episodes, of two middle entries and a final group of entries in, if possible, stretto, and a conclusion. In the circumstances there is no time for cleverness or experiment: what is to be done must be clear-cut and the candidate has to be writing confidently all the time.

One diploma in this subject requires also a thesis of not more than five thousand words, to be sent beforehand, on a subject chosen from three that are set. The broad material for this can be got from books, but it must show original thought and opinion as well as a practical knowledge of the works of the period, which ought to be used for purposes of illustration. It will naturally be expressed in graceful literary style and should be typewritten.

There may be, in addition, exercises in dictation, including a melody, two melodic parts, four-part chords, and modulations. In the two melodic parts test it is necessary on the first hearing to seize with pencil dots on the stave as much as possible, the upper part and the rhythm probably first, then the lower part, the note values, the barring. It is of the utmost importance to get the first notes correct, otherwise everything will be wrong. With the four-part chords, the outside parts are most readily recognized and should be dotted down, with figures below for the two or three chords requiring them.

With the repetitions of the passage, corrections are made and the chords filled in. In a progression like this:

it would not be bad to write the second tenor note as A instead of D: the one thing to be said against it is that, one of the notes of the chord having to be duplicated, the candidate is not recognizing which note it is and that the doubling is at the unison instead of the octave.

The viva voce part of the examination calls for a knowledge of the compasses and capabilities of voices and instruments; the history of English music for a set period, a prescribed orchestral score; also playing from vocal score (including the C clefs for alto and tenor), a figured or unfigured bass, the harmonizing of a melody, completing an unfinished musical sentence and modulating between specified keys; and discussing methods of teaching.

The questions on history will be outside the subject of the thesis, and the best way to meet them is to make a synopsis with headings of the main events of the period and memorize them. Here again a practical familiarity with the works that exerted an influence on musical progress is necessary, and a brief opportunity to demonstrate it is given. The discussion of the orchestral score may apply to its form, its subjects and their development, the keys of the different movements, unusual features of expression, the orchestral effects and their special characteristics, their variety in repetition. The score chosen will always afford sufficient scope for enlightened analysis.

The four-part vocal score calls for diligent practice from various publications of such music and special care for the inner C clefs, particularly when they share in the crossing of parts. Like the other practical tests, this has to be played straight off and in time. In the harmonization of a bass or a melody, it often happens that the beginning of the given part suggests the major key and proves towards the end to be in the minor; and then it is too late to make amends. It is therefore very necessary to make sure of the key by looking at the last bar. This with cadences, a possible modulation in the middle, and any other individual points have all to be decided within the time of the brief glance which is permitted. The other outside part must be interesting: if the melody, it should move with purpose and reach a climax. This means looking ahead. The harmonies are to be of simple context and not change unnecessarily. But plain chords are not wanted; there should be passing-notes, prepared discords, suspensions, and appoggiaturas; watch must be kept for sequences; a long note is to be accompanied by moving parts; imitations and the occasional relief of rests will be effective, while the interest should increase towards the end. The avoidance of consecutives will have become instinctive to a candidate whose whole work is concerned with it. Additional facility in this spontaneous test at the piano can be acquired by writing out harmonizations around a given alto or tenor part. The test in modulations implies that the original key will be well authenticated by at least four bars before the first move away from it. Imitations and sequences should if possible be introduced: that is, the exercise is to have character.

The questions on teaching are such as to ascertain the candidate's experience. He should base his work on ear training, and will be required to explain as to a student the formation of chords and their inversions and cadences, their logical succession one after another (often a difficulty with young people), the reasons for the rules of part-writing, the origins of diatonic and chromatic discords, suspensions, modulations, passing and auxiliary notes, the five species of strict counterpoint and with the licences of free counterpoint their

H

influence on composition, the musical forms and their various treatments by the great composers. He will also be given exercises to criticize at the piano. Further experience from hearing and exploring music as well as attending concerts is necessary for the identification of well-known standard works played by the examiner.

It is to be noted that the successful candidate has to have not only a knowledge of the theoretical side of music, as the title of his diploma attests, but has had to prove that he is able to share it for the good of others, and that he can play sufficiently well to bring real life into his teaching. Though as a theoretician he might tend to be detached from the main stream of musical activity, he is also a practitioner eager to impart to his students the viewpoint, of which they so often stand in need, that they and their works are not dedicated apart but can be of value only when they are in touch with the more progressive aspects of their art.

Diplomas in Composition

A DIPLOMA in composition is based on that in theory, but it calls for the submission of original work, which must be the candidate's unaided endeavour. The paper examination is more advanced, as is the viva voce, which includes a discussion of the original work. Much that has been said of other diplomas, especially the Fellowship of the Royal College of Organists, applies to it. It is, however, designed for those with a natural gift for advanced musical expression, and is a highly specialized challenge to put all theory into practical results that can stand expert criticism and be performed to the public satisfaction. In many ways it offers a good foundation for a university degree in music.

The work submitted, which must be for chorus and orchestra, should include examples of the various subjects included in the paper examination, extending to double counterpoint, canon, and fugue. The writing of them will therefore serve a double purpose in fulfilling a requirement and in providing admirable practice towards working the paper. They might well be included in a cantata of several movements of different characters. The first could be an introduction or overture for orchestra; then a four- or five-part chorus, with words and orchestral accompaniment, followed by an example of two voices in canon, two in one, with a free part added, which might be accompanied by strings. Then a vocal solo, again with full orchestra, as also will be the closing number, a fugue for four voices, including various examples of double counterpoint at the octave or fifteenth. The words could be chosen to give the work a unity of purpose, and they have to be carefully indicated below each voice.

The candidate is not troubled, as so often in real life, by local considerations as to the resources of the orchestra; money and limited talent do not enter into it, and he should plan for the symphonic proportions of strings, two flutes, two oboes, two clarinets, two bassoons, two horns, two trumpets, three trombones, and timpani, the customary forces latterly used by Beethoven. The clarinets and the trumpets will probably be in B flat, the horns in F, the timpani for the tonic and dominant. By placing each couple of instruments on one stave, the first and second trombones on one and the third on another, he will have a full score of fourteen staves. It will be more easily read if the bar lines are drawn down in three groups, one for the wood-wind, one for the brass and timpani, the third for the strings, and at the beginning of each page these groups should be further emphasized by square brackets. After the first page, abbreviations of the instrumental names should be entered on every left-hand one, but there is no need to repeat the clefs and key signatures. The music for each movement should be drafted out in ink in piano score, carrying such suggestions of the orchestra as may occur and probably inspire its progress. And, of course, the orchestration will be begun only after the movement is completely and finally outlined.

The most profitable way of learning to write for the orchestra is by combining the study of scores with hearing their effects in actual performance. Thus does the student find that what may seem unpromising to the eye is successful to the ear, is able to probe the reason for it, and marvel how is brought to pass many a thing that would have appeared impossible. He should note how the composer supports the balance between the different groups, how he achieves his delicate colourings, how he builds up a crescendo, reduces it in a diminuendo, gets certain timbres of chording, how amidst such abundance he prevents an over-fullness but preserves clarity, and thus fulfils what is the one chief rule in an endlessly varied art. The candidate's introduction offers him the opportunity of giving effect to his study and experience. It should be sufficiently expansive to reveal his material and its manner of treatment. In it he is free to put any amount of detail, individual touches arising from the relationships of the forces, the use of solo instruments, of soft brass, of the full power with which they can all combine.

In the rest of the work the orchestra acts the part of accompanist, which means that in writing for it the chorus will always have to be given first consideration. Its effects will be broader, with less opportunity for detail. It must not be simply doubling the voices. When they are in their most vigorous moods they must be given a solid background of support; when singing in a whisper they might be better without any accompaniment at all. But between these extremes there is still for the orchestra an infinite variety of purposeful shading. It will be complementary, playing a subtly independent part, adding notes to the chording, filling in the harmony, altering repetitions, lending a helping hand to the voices in their limitations. Advantage too can be taken of the tonal differences between the two forces so that they may go their own certain ways to combine in dissonant notes quite effectively.

In the solo song, the accompaniment must even more consider the singer to enable him to make his words audible through the surrounding body of tone. It is safer to avoid the upper reaches of the wood-wind and give every chance to the delicacy of the strings; for the strings can do anything that is asked of them. It is to them an independent melody will generally be allotted in preference to the wood-wind. The brass have to be employed with great reserve and usually to give effect to their power of quickly working up a crescendo. Here especially in the difficult adjustment of two unequal forces will the candidate derive every benefit by listening to a singer accompanied by an accomplished orchestrator. In the fugue, where the voices are of equal importance, the orchestra doubles them at the same pitch and the octave, while also supplying the harmonic framework. A contrapuntal independent part, or two parts at the most, is effective though fraught with danger, for through it all the flow of fugal parts must be recognizable. Here once again clarity is the prime necessity.

The combination of voices and orchestra has become a distinctly personal art since the Olympian days of Bach and Handel, and for his emancipation the candidate must have familiarized himself with the more elusive and impressionist methods of modern composers. They breathe more the freedom of the open air and of travel abroad. The early works of Elgar, *The Revenge* of Stanford, *Toward the Unknown Region* by Vaughan Williams, and many others, are such as to lead him on the way he should go. These he ought to copy and try to emulate, so that by developing what he has to say, and finding a contemporary expression for it, he will be prepared to meet the requirements.

In him do we have a leader among diploma holders, one who has received the call of his art, has subjected himself to its disciplines, and has been accepted; one who goes forth on his life's purpose, and that purpose higher than any other, to be a music maker and a dreamer of dreams.

INDEX

INDEX

DATE DUE

GAYLORD

PRINTED IN U.S.A.